BaHa

Our Pride and Joy

APA PUBLICATIONS
Part of the Langenscheidt Publishing Group

L

New Providence

3.2 km / 2 miles

N o r t h e a s t   P r o v i d e n c e   C h a n n e l

Salt Cay

Hanover Sound

The Narrows

Athol Island

Cabbage Island

CABBAGE BEACH

Paradise Isl. Golf Course

Paradise Island

Sea Gardens

Paradise (Hog) Island

PARADISE BEACH

MONTAGU BEACH

Dick's Point

Fort Montagu

Prop Deck

Yacht Haven

Rawson Sq.

Hospital

Queen's College

Creek Village

Blackbirds Tower

Camperdown

East End Point

Culberts Point

YAMACRAW BEACH

Port New Providence

Winton Heights

Winton Meadows

Winton

Eastern Estates

Fox Hill

Fox Hill Village

Sandilands Village

St. Augustines Monastery

Yamacraw Hill Estates

Yamacraw Hill Road

29

Nassau East

Gardens

Village S.C.

Queens Park

Prince Charles

Mall on the Marathon

Englerston

Regency Park

Glendiston

Kensington Gardens

South Garden Estates

Pinewood Gardens Estates

Malcolm Creek

Long Point

W h i t e   B a n k

SOUTH BEACH

South Beach Estate West

South Beach Estate East

South Beach Rd.

Golden Gates S.C.

Golden Gates

Sunshine Park

Harold Pond

Millar Heights

Bonefish Pond

Cay Point

Guana Cay

Fishing Cays

Millars Sound

Millars Boat Harbour

Millars Rum Plant

Bacardi Rum Distillery

Cow Pen Road

Campground

Gladstone Road

Carmichael Village

NEW PROVIDENCE

Coral Heights

Shopping Centre

Coral Harbour Road

Coral Harbour

Coral Harbour Golf Course

Royal Bahamas Defence Base

Ocean Hole

Adelaide Rd.

Adelaide Road

Adelaide

Adelaide Village

South West Bay

ADELAIDE BEACH

Fleeming Point

Sound

Nassau International Airport

Windsor Field

Lake Cunningham

Lake Killarney

36

35

Stapleton Gardens

Wilson Pond

Oakes Field Airfield

Oakes Field Golf Course

Town Mall

Government Building

Chippingham

Greater Oakes Field

Seafloor Aquarium

The Grove

NASSAU

Fort Fincastle

Fort Charlotte

Rosetta

Gowen House

Goodman's Point

Brown's Point

Silver Cay

Ambassador G.C.

Stephania Gale

Hobby Horse Race Track

Cable Beach

CABLE BEACH

SAUNDERS BEACH

COLONIAL BEACH

Straw Market

Fort Start

Arawak Cay

Long Cay

North Cay

Delaporte Point

Rock Point

The Caves

28

John F. Kennedy Drive

Gambier Village

Road

Tropical Gardens

LOVE BEACH

Northwest Point

Old Fort Point

Old Fort Bay

Old Fort

Windsor Field

Coral Gardens

Creek Point

Mt. Pleasant Marina

Lyford Cay

Lyford Cay Golf Course

Mt. Pleasant

West Bay Street

20

Mt. Pleasant

29

South West St.

Clifton Pier

Old Fort (Ruins)

Clifton Bay

Clifton House (Ruins)

Clifton Bluff

Clifton Point

Simms Point

Welcome!

A scattering of some 2,700 coral-based pearls of land between the Atlantic and the Caribbean, the Bahamas comprise enough romantic islands to last any traveller a lifetime. Only 30 of the islands are inhabited, and of these, even the busiest are still extremely peaceful by Continental standards.

 'Having been raised in a quiet farming and fishing community in Canada, I found adjustment to Bahamian island life practically effortless,' says **Deby Nash**, Insight's correspondent in the Bahamas. Deby has lived in Nassau since 1986, working as a teacher and journalist. The city, she says, is remarkably international. 'The streets are filled with people from every corner of the world, the shops are stocked with international fragrances and fashions, and Nassuvians are as stylish as any residents of cities ten times Nassau's size.'

Deby has aimed to illustrate some of the diversity of Nassau in her city itinerary in this book. But she has also designed other itineraries which will reveal the seductive, slow pace of island life, concentrating on the key destinations of New Providence, Paradise Island, Grand Bahama and its city of Freeport, Eleuthera, Harbour Island and Spanish Wells.

Wherever you go, you will be welcome, and if you follow the itineraries in this book you will enjoy the highlights of the Bahamas, together with the simple hospitality and open-door warmth of the islands' residents.

C O N T E N T S

Pages 2/3:
The island
of Exuma

Pages 8/9:
Lady Masons of
Holmes Rock,
Grand Bahama

Shopping, Dining & Nightlife

Calendar of Events

Practical Information

Maps

HISTORY & CULTURE

Lucayans and Legacies

A confused Christopher Columbus stumbled on to San Salvador Island on October 12, 1492. It was obvious he had not found a shortcut to China as he had set out to do. The graceful, gentle, brown-skinned Indians who met him on shore bore no resemblance to the Orientals he had expected. The disappointed navigator would never know that this land of 'shallow seas', the Bahamas, was to become the gateway to a New World — one of riches beyond anyone's imaginings.

The Lucayan Indians had tended their islands in peace and tranquillity for more than 500 years before Columbus, but now that they were discovered, they would soon be gone forever. The skilled fishermen — once perhaps 4,000 strong — had no resistance to the European diseases Columbus and company brought with them. A key decider in their downfall was the thin topsoil on these limestone and coral-based islands: because the land yielded neither gold nor bountiful harvests of fruits and vegetables, the Spanish decided that

Lucayan Indians hunting giant turtles

the islanders would have to compensate them with human labour. The brief notes most history books accord the Lucayans mention that they were 'recruited' by the Spanish to work in the nearby mines of Hispaniola (now Haiti and the Dominican Republic). Many would die during the sea voyage. Depopulation through disease and slavery continued until little more than 25 years later, when the Lucayans were finally no more.

Columbus arrives

With the labour force depleted, and neither gold nor treasures to be had, the Bahamas would remain deserted for almost 100 years. Only Ponce de Leon, while looking for the fountain of youth, passed through the islands, including San Salvador. In 1513 he touched on what is today called Grand Bahama. He wrote in his journals of a fast-moving, warm current flowing past the islands: this turned out to be the Gulf Stream, which would eventually lead his ship to the coast of Florida.

A Growing Sanctuary

Settlement in this New World began in earnest only in the 17th century, and once again for all the wrong reasons. The British, like the Spanish, had recognised a potential in the region for creating fortunes for themselves – not from land, but from the misfortunes of others. The slave trade was now in Africans. And poor or no experience in navigation, paired with treacherous shoals and well-armed galleons, made piracy a low-maintenance, high-return business. Rival slavers stole readily from each other.

The early 1600s was also a time of religious turmoil. The Anglican Church had been founded by Henry VIII, and British Puritan Congregationists, who acknowledged no higher power than the Bible or God, were looking for somewhere to practise their religion without fear.

William Sayle, a Puritan former governor of Bermuda, was among those who set sail seeking religious freedom. With few navigational skills, some 70 of his crew were shipwrecked off the north coast of Eleuthera. To this day, you will find a cave in North Eleuthera where these Eleutheran Adventurers are said to have gathered for shelter and prayers.

But the land had not improved, and the Puritans found it hard to survive. Many of them, including Sayle, were forced to leave. He returned to Bermuda in 1657, but came back frequently to the

Bahamas, still looking for a permanent settlement. One island he discovered had excellent potential, particularly with its natural harbour. This was New Providence, on which the city of Nassau is now located, and thanks to development by Sayle it was to become the magnet of the Caribbean for the next 350 years.

Early Nassau

More and more Bermudian Puritans began moving to New Providence from Eleuthera as word spread that the farming and fishing were easier there. The island community continued to grow, though plagued by lawlessness. It soon became a base for piracy, the slave trade, and cannibalising shipwrecked galleons. Even the notorious pirate Blackbeard is said to have been a frequent Nassau visitor.

A female pirate

In the territorial tug-of-war between England and Spain, New Providence was attacked as many as four times in 25 years, and Nassau was burned to the ground by the Spaniards.

Eventually the British got the upper hand and in 1718 Captain Woodes Rogers, Royal Governor, arrived to take control of the colony which was now under the direct authority of the Crown. During his tenure, he accurately predicted that he would be remembered because 'he expelled the pirates and restored commerce.'

Prejudice and Politics

Woodes Rogers also put in place the first steps towards a representative Bahamian Assembly. Bahamians, like their neighbours to the north, the North American colonists, had had no representation in government. Their lives until then had been directly controlled by British agents of the Crown. The first representative Assembly was convened in 1729, and thereafter rarely missed a session, making it one of the longest continually meeting assemblies in the New World.

The issue of colour was becoming increasingly important on the islands. The representative Assembly appeared to represent only the narrow interests of powerful Nassuvians, who were mostly of European extraction and therefore white. But the black population was increasing fast, and Bahamians of African descent were finding that no matter what country they came from, they had one major factor uniting them: oppression by the white minority.

Britain outlawed slavery at home in 1772, but the new liberty took time to spread to the Bahamas. As the fires of revolution mounted in the 13 American colonies, men with religious and ideological convictions made their way to the Bahamas once again. Among them was Frank Spence, a slave who arrived in 1780 with a group of British Loyalists. He saved up enough money to buy his freedom a year later, and eventually began the first Baptist congregation in the Bahamas.

Loyalists and Emancipation

At the end of the American War of Independence in 1783, the terms of the Treaty of Versailles included the British exchange of Florida for the Bahamas. The losing Loyalists fled north and south; those who came to the Bahamas brought with them thousands of slaves, and were briefly successful at establishing cotton plantations. However, this love affair with the land was once again to be short-lived as problems quickly developed with insect infestation, overplanting, and deforestation.

In 1807 the slave trade was prohibited throughout all British possessions and on British ships, and the British navy began to free slaves on those vessels they captured, adding considerable numbers to the former plantation slaves living on the islands. This growing population now had a country, and even property, but few skills and few options to relocate. After all, America was still adjusting to its new status, and its uneasy truce between the races held few prospects for immigrants. As a result some freed men made their homes in New Providence, but many preferred the isolation and relative lack of interference in the Out Islands, today called the Family Islands. These people integrated relatively well with the original white settlers, largely because the latter had been cut off from European influence. In isolation, often with slaves as their only company, these first white Bahamian settlers had developed a relationship based on mutual survival and respect. The legacy, centuries later, is the unique character of the Bahamian people.

But the American Civil War (1861-1865) saw the return of smuggling to the Bahamas. With the growing number of lighthouses, shipwrecks were fewer and thus becoming less profitable. Bahamians were asked to show their support for Abraham Lincoln by blockading the

British Loyalist Andrew Deveaux

Unloading cotton in 1865

southern ports to stop black-market activity. But easy money was to be had from smuggling, and stopping it wasn't easy. Fast boats smuggled goods to Florida – to consumers who, ironically, had only recently been the slave-masters of their new suppliers.

With peace and the signing of the Apomattox Treaty in 1865 the fragile Bahamas economy once again took a sharp downturn. For a while, the humble but legitimate sponging industry briefly became the country's largest money-earner. But bigger dollars were to be had elsewhere. Many skilled Bahamians contracted themselves out to citrus farms and plantations in the United States, especially in the Florida area. The exodus was to continue until the tourism boom of the 1950s. Many contract workers never returned, creating a family bond between Florida and the Bahamas that continues even today.

Prohibition and the Windsors

For those Bahamians who remained at home, the US Prohibition laws of 1920 created instant prosperity. Bootlegging on the high seas made for good business. And bars with free-flowing liquor attracted the adventurous, creating the Bahamas' jazz age of the 1930s.

Prohibition was repealed in 1933. Once more, it looked like the 'in' place would soon be on its way out of favour. But with World War II, the arrival of the Duke and Duchess of Windsor in 1940, following the former's abdication from the British throne, focused world attention back on the Bahamas. The man who had given up his crown for the woman he loved lent an air of sophistication and – albeit tinged – respectability to the tiny colony.

Black and white Bahamians alike volunteered to serve in the Canadian and British West Indies forces. The British and American high command chose a deserted section of the western part of New Providence to construct an enormous pilot training centre for the war effort. Black construction workers became incensed when they found they were being paid less than white men working on the same project. In one of few public displays of violence in the country's history, they rioted on Bay Street, the bastion of the establishment. Several were killed in clashes, and offices and bar rooms were looted or burned to the ground. The workers eventually secured their raise, and the airbase was eventually built. After the war it became Nassau international Airport.

The Windsors in Nassau

At about the same time – 1942 – Canadian-born gold magnate and philanthropist Sir Harry Oakes was brutally murdered. With the Duke of Windsor overseeing the investigation, charges were soon laid against Oakes's son-in-law. After a sensational trial, the accused was acquitted. Today, the case of the murder of one of the richest men in the British Empire still remains unsolved.

From Colony to Commonwealth

And then the war was over. It seemed everyone was seeking ways to escape the harsh realities of a post-war adjustment. Many Bahamians were still working as farm labourers in the US, but the opportunities were becoming scarce.

Meanwhile, an invasion of another sort was taking place back home. British investors began buying up huge chunks of Bahamas real estate as fears of increased taxation grew with the election of the British Labour Party. And, closer at hand, Americans, who now had both the desire and the means to travel, were discovering the Bahamas could be a fast and inexpensive weekend getaway.

Sensing a trend, astute businessman Sir Stafford Sands created a National Development Board in 1950, which would market the Bahamas as a year-round vacation spot. Nassau's harbour was dredged to provide docking to even the largest ships in the expanding Caribbean cruise-ship market.

Sands also helped put in place bank secrecy laws comparable to those of Switzerland, with attractive tax concessions that would establish the Bahamas as an international banking centre. For the first time in centuries, two industries – tourism and offshore banking – ensured a legitimate and promising future for Bahamians. They continue even today to provide the Bahamas with the second highest per capita income (the Cayman Islands boasts the highest) in the region.

The new-found affluence of the early 1960s coincided with the rise of party politics. Women won the right to vote in 1962, and they were a significant force in the creation of the Progressive Liberal Party (PLP) by Bahamians of African descent. The PLP became an alternative to the United Bahamian Party (UBP), which consisted mostly of wealthy white Bahamian businessmen known as the 'Bay Street Boys'.

Queen Elizabeth II with Gerald Cash and Sir Lynden Pindling

Lynden Pindling's PLP won the 1967 election with the largest number of voters ever enfranchised: a black majority government had been won without bloodshed or outside interference. So began the 'Quiet Revolution' – the non-violent philosophy of the PLP to bring in majority rule. Two years later the Constitution was revised, and Pindling became the first Prime Minister.

By the early 1970s, the UBP had aligned itself with splinter groups and become the Free National Movement. They agreed to assist the PLP in negotiating the terms of the nation's first independent constitution. On July 10, 1973, after 325 years as a colony and possession of Britain, the Bahamas achieved independence.

Prime Minister Pindling was knighted by the Queen in 1983, but his government's travel and tourism explosion had brought with it some negative side-effects, notably in the trade of cocaine, for which the Bahamas are ideally positioned. Close cooperation with American drug enforcement agencies has stemmed the tide.

Investment in tourist infrastructure has been huge. Nassau's Crystal Palace Resort and Casino cost $300 million before it opened in 1990. In the same year, the International Business Act became law, giving the Bahamas a special place in offshore banking.

On August 19, 1992, the opposition Free National Movement, with slogans like 'Deliverance' and 'Government in the Sunshine', became the Bahamas' second administration, breaking the 25-year-hold of the Progressive Liberal Party.

Days later, Hurricane Andrew cut a devastating swath through the nation, hitting the island of Eleuthera particularly hard. In less than 48 hours, new Prime Minister Hubert Ingraham's hurricane relief committee was already hard at work. Barely a year later, the restoration process was practically complete to typically high standards.

Nassau's Crystal Palace

Historical Highlights

1492 Columbus arrives in the New World, at the island of Guanahani. He renames it San Salvador ('Holy Saviour').

1513 Ponce de Leon does not find the fountain of youth, but does discover the Gulf Stream.

1647 Eleutheran Adventurers create the first republic of the New World.

1648 Cigatoo Island claimed by colonials and renamed Eleuthera, from the Greek word meaning Freedom.

1718 Britain sends Woodes Rogers as Royal Governor, to combat growing piracy and lawlessness in the new colony.

1729 The first representative Assembly was convened.

1772 Slavery is outlawed in Britain but not throughout the empire as a whole.

1776 First foreign invasion, by the United States, at Fort Montague.

1780 Frank Spence, a slave, arrives with a group of Loyalists. He goes on to create a ministry that becomes the Bahamian Anglican Church.

1782 The second foreign invasion – the Spanish. They recapture the Bahamas as retribution for persistent piracy against their vessels.

1783 Immigration of American Loyalists after the Treaty of Versailles. Other Loyalists flee to Nova Scotia, Canada, where today's predominantly black Acadia University remains a popular choice among the many Bahamian students intent on studying abroad.

1793 Fort Fincastle built at New Providence's highest point.

1834 Slavery abolished throughout the British Empire, including the Bahamas.

1861–5 The Royal Victoria Hotel is built during the economic boom generated from smuggling goods to Florida during the American Civil War. After the war the economy takes a downturn.

1920–33 Rum-running and the Jazz Age flourish in the Bahamas during Prohibition until its repealing in 1933. This begins the prominence of the 'Bay Street Boys'.

1940s Fame and glamour return to the Bahamas as the Duke and Duchess of Windsor arrive.

1942 The murder of Canadian-born gold magnate and philanthropist Sir Harry Oakes.

1955 Wallace Groves, founder of the Grand Bahama Port Authority, designs and gets approval for the Hawksbill Creek Agreement, creating a tax-free haven which will become Freeport-Lucaya.

1960s Growth of black consciousness and creation of the Progressive Liberal Party (PLP).

1962 Women win the right to vote and are important in the creation of the Progressive Liberal Party (PLP).

1967 PLP wins elections and begins the 'Quiet Revolution' towards majority rule.

1973 On 10 July, Bahamas achieves independence.

1977 Government introduces Bahamas' first radio and television broadcasting system.

1982 Janet Bostwick becomes first female member of Parliament.

1983 Prime minister Pindling is knighted by the Queen.

1990 Opening of the Crystal Palace Resort and Casino.

1992 On 19 August, the Free National Movement wins decisively over the Pindling government, becoming the first new administration in 25 years. Special quincentennial celebrations are held in San Salvador.

1994 The Bahamas comes of age as it celebrates its 21st anniversary.

The Bahamas

80 km / 50 miles

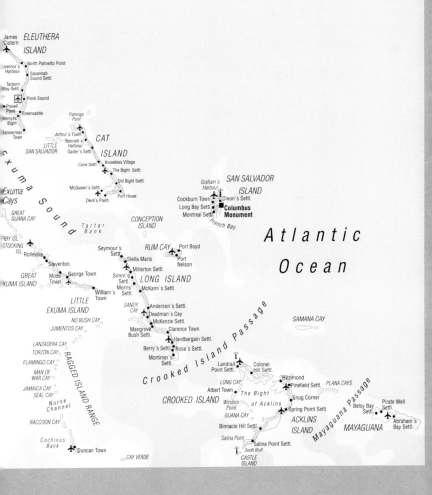

New Providence & Paradise

Only 200 miles (60km) from the Florida coastline, the island of New Providence is a half hour's flying time from Miami, 45 minutes from Fort Lauderdale, and one hour from Palm Beach. At 22 miles (35km) long and 7 miles (11km) wide, this former shipping colony has an infrastructure intended for horse and buggies only – as will quickly become apparent to any visitor. The traffic congestion, however, is worthy of any big city, and many of the streets are without street signs. It's best left to your cab or jitney driver to take you around the inner city of Nassau, as they know which streets are one- or two-way (not all are marked).

Most cruise ships dock at Nassau

Public transport is the jitney – a 32-seat Bahamian public bus. As an alternative to hiring your own taxi, you can always rent a motorcycle. By restricting your exploration to Bay Street, a main road which flows east and west along the shoreline, you can get to see most of the island without worrying about becoming lost.

The 75-cent fare on a jitney is simplest. Be sure you have coins for the fare; jitney drivers will not give change. They can get you to most points of the island, but they cease operation after 6pm. Evening forays must be made by taxi (ask the fare before setting off) or by transport which is regularly arranged by the hotels to the more popular spots.

A hands-on-heart smile

1. Downtown Nassau

A horse and buggy ('surrey') ride and walking tour of Nassau's inner city, replete with international shops and boutiques, including the House of Parliament and the Straw Market.

The pulse of the city is Bay Street, Nassau's oldest and main thoroughfare. Taste a hearty traditional breakfast of boiled fish and johnny cake at the **Palm Restaurant**, located on Bay Street central, at the very core of the city.

Just one block away, at **Rawson Square**, is the starting point for the horse and buggy tours and the main tourist office. A bust of the first Bahamian Governor-General, Sir Milo Butler, is a popular photo opportunity here.

A surrey ride

Then hop on a **surrey** – some actually have a fringe on top – and at from $5 per person, have a Bahamahost-trained driver take you on a half-hour tour of the downtown area. The half-hour tour will provide you with a cultural and historical synopsis of the streets and buildings along the route, as well as identifying the flora and fauna indigenous to the Bahamas. Though the traffic might make you feel a bit apprehensive, neither the horses nor the Nassau car drivers seem to be nervous in each other's company, even in the rush hour. This tour is the perfect way to get an overview of the city centre.

The landmarks appear quickly in this small central area. The first of these is the **Garden of Remembrance**, which is located in Parliament Square, just off Parliament Street. With court-houses on one side, and the Nassau Public Library on the other, this tiny area is actually a cenotaph, commemorating the Bahamians who died in World Wars I and II.

After the surrey turns on to Shirley Street, which is second only to Bay Street in the amount of traffic, you'll see the **Nassau Public Library** on your left. Built in 1797, this octagonal-shaped build-

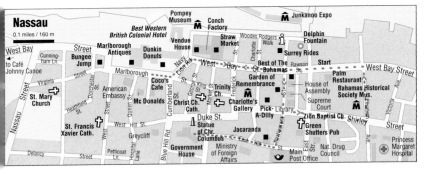

Nassau Public Library

ing was formerly a jail. The library is still surrounded by small courtrooms, and you'll probably see some clients sitting under the shade of a tree as they wait for their cases to be called. If you decide to browse around on your own, it would be worth the visit to go inside the library. About a dozen of what used to be prison cells are now lined with books. The librarian will also show you a rare collection of historical prints, colonial artefacts, and the Bahamian Collection – volumes written by and about Bahamians.

On the same side of Shirley Street, two blocks along and at the corner of Elizabeth Avenue, is the Bahamas **Historical Society Museum**. It has several displays depicting Bahamas history from pre-Columbus – including Lucayan Indian artefacts – to the present. One block farther down, on the right side of Shirley Street, is the **Princess Margaret Hospital**, the public hospital so named in honour of the Princess's visit in 1955.

The surrey will make a left turn for a short trot down Bay Street, and take you back to where you began. When you step out of the carriage, you'll be looking at **Rawson** and **Parliament** squares, which contain the main Bahamian government offices. These include the House of Parliament, the Old Colonial Secretary Office, and the Supreme Court. You may want to sit in on a session in the latter and witness the old British system of justice in operation. A statue of Queen Victoria sits regally in the centre of Parliament Square. This is a popular area for performances by visiting musicians and musical groups.

Turn right (west) on to Bay Street and take a leisurely stroll past the duty-free fashion and jewellery shops. Just a few short

Parliament Square

blocks away, in the Market Plaza, is the Nassau **Straw Market**, a national landmark covering a full city block. First constructed in 1901, it was destroyed by fire in 1974 and replaced by the present structure. Almost any handicraft you can imagine is to be found amongst the 500 stalls at this market, but most common are items made of straw or wood. Your best souvenir will be straw-work done by vendors on the spot. Though haggling is frowned on in most storefront retail establishments, almost all prices here are negotiable. Be sure to walk through both the lower and the upper levels; on most days, a local entertainer will be performing in the central courtyard of the second terrace.

The **Pompey Museum** is practically next door. The present museum and art gallery was once used in the 18th century for slave auctions. Today its artefacts and historical documents trace slavery, abolition, and emancipation. The second storey contains paintings by Amos Ferguson, the Bahamas' renowned and oldest living artist. Between the Pompey Museum and the Straw Market is the **Conch Factory**, which sells watches and jewellery made from the popular shell. The workmanship is of exceptional quality, and you can also find here many lovely pieces fashioned from coral.

In the Straw Market

Follow the bend in the road, past the Sheraton Best Western British Colonial Hotel, to **Coco's Cafe**. With pale pastel decor and soothing jazz or *soca* coming through the unobtrusive sound system, it has a calming effect, especially if you have a light salad or seafood lunch while watching the noonday crowds pass by.

After lunch, retrace your steps along Bay Street. You'll see several duty-free shops, with a wide selection of exclusive perfumes and designer fashions. Turn right at Parliament Street and watch members of Parliament and barristers moving busily between the courts and the House of Parliament, lying just behind the statue of Queen Victoria.

At the top of Parliament Street is the **Main Post Office**. There is no home mail delivery in the Bahamas; the thousands of metal postboxes you see are a valuable commodity, as residents can sometimes wait for more than a year for one to become available for rental. The Post Office mounts displays of arts, crafts, or historical events which are changed regularly. There are also special collectors' editions of stamps which make great souvenirs.

Government House

You can see the entrance to **Government House** from the Post Office steps. It is the Bahamas' version of Buckingham Palace, and the official residence of the Governor-General, the Queen's official representative in the islands. Two Defence Force officers, in white military dress, are at their ceremonial post at the gates at the entrance. Just past them, a white statue of Christopher Columbus stands on the steps of the House.

As you walk back down Parliament Street from the Post Office you might want to stop of and try some beer on tap at the 'velly British' **Green Shutters Pub**. It's situated across the street from the **National Drug Council**, repository of one of the most innovative and comprehensive research collections available on Aids in the Caribbean region. The council's offices are open to the general public.

Near the bottom of the hill, not far from where you began your day in Nassau, is the **Pick-A-Dilly Restaurant**, housed in the Parliament Hotel. With its own Daiquiri bar, it offers comfortable indoor or outdoor seating. Its location also makes it a regular meeting place for Parliamentarians and attorneys who like to hold their 'power' luncheons here. An acoustic group serenades as you dine on anything from fresh seafood to nachos and salsa. A traditional British tea for two – complete with finger cucumber sandwiches and banana bread – is available in the afternoons. In the evenings there is also a live local band who will get you on your feet to test your *meringue* dance steps.

If you'd like a little more local flavour (and tempo) for your evening, I recommend you try **Ronnie's Rebel Room**, located just inside the entrance to the Nassau Beach Hotel, on Cable Beach. The headliner at this recently renovated nightclub is the Bahamian recording artist Ronnie Butler; he and his vibrant band play continuous Bahamanian and Caribbean rhythms right through until the early hours of the morning.

Cocktails at Pick-A-Dilly

2. To Paradise Island

A day that starts in Nassau and moves on to the 'Monaco of the Caribbean'. End the itinerary back on New Providence, in the Caribbean's largest casino, which is located on Cable Beach.

Nassau's character has probably been moulded more by visitors to its shores than most countries. Nowhere is the impact of tourism more evident than in the heart of town. Just behind where the downtown surreys are stationed stands a signpost with arrows pointing in all directions. It graces the entrance to the **Tourist Information Centre**, which has every brochure and bulletin available about what there is to see on this and any other Bahamian island.

Paradise Island viewed from a plane

Beside it, and parallel to Bay Street – as well as stretching half its downtown length – is the **Woodes Rogers Walk**. You should begin your day here by watching for a while the magnificent cruise ships that regularly glide in and out along the waterfront. **Prince George Dock**, the largest port in the Caribbean, bustles with nonstop traffic as cruise ships from around the world jostle for berths every morning, their passengers pouring into the city in their thousands.

As you stroll along the walkway, you'll encounter vendors who arrived before sunrise to set up their stalls here or at the Straw

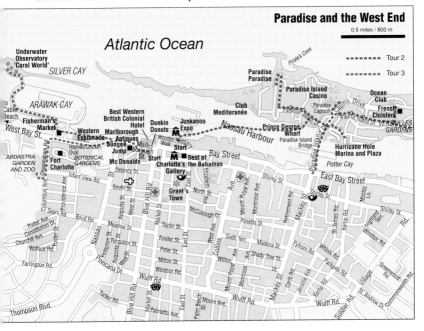

Crystal Palace Beach

Market further along. The market has rows and rows of colourful straw-work, including hats, place mats, dolls, and baskets, along with elaborate wood carvings, and, of course, mounds of T-shirts. The vendors do a bustling business selling fresh fruits and the morning's catch, and will plait your hair into cornrows if you want to 'look Bahamian'.

Every half hour or so, a glass-bottom boat loads up here, with passengers about to make a trip to visit the Sea Gardens — a protected marine park with a large variety of fish and corals. But you should be looking out for a different form of marine transport: at the same docking area is the **Paradise Island ferry**, which shuttles guests to the island every 20 minutes, starting at 8am. The ferry route takes you to a number of points on Paradise Island, and then offers a return trip to the Straw Market or the cruise ship dock.

Sometimes called the 'Monaco of the Caribbean', **Paradise Island** had much humbler origins than its celestial title may suggest: the 826-acre (335-ha) retreat was called Hog Island by its early settlers, specifically because at one time the island was mainly a home for pigs, with not much else going on.

How things have changed. Cruising yachtsmen can dock at the 57-slip, full-service Hurricane Hole Marina, and tourists also arrive at Paradise Island International Airport. The island has championship golf and tennis courts spread through its six major hotels and condo properties, and has more than 1,000 hotel rooms.

You may have to be a millionaire to live on Paradise Island, but there are no such restrictions for the tourist. It's truly a pedestrian's paradise, with quaint gift shops scattered throughout. At any of the hotels you can catch a courtesy Little Switzerland shuttle, which connects all the Paradise Island hotels and will take you to and from the boutiques and shops at **Hurricane Hole Plaza**, which — unsurprisingly — has the biggest **Little Switzerland** duty-free store on the island.

Shopping over, stroll along any of the white sandy beaches, which are within easy walking distance once you're on the island. The clean white sand goes on forever, and is becoming a popular place for moviemakers who want beautiful beach scenes with blue waves rippling into the sunsets. Try to end up at the west end of the island, on Paradise Beach, by which time you'll be ready for something to eat.

Conch, prepared Bahamian-style, is the island speciality, and Bahamians pride themselves on preparing variations of even the same recipe. Fritters, for example, can be made with either minced or chopped conch. I prefer the 'conchy' chopped conch, with coarsely chopped bits mixed into the spicy batter, though there are some who'd rather savour the more subtle, ground-up version. You can get some conchy conch fritters and a decadent dessert of guava duff at the outdoor cafe of the sports-inclusive **Paradise Paradise**. Use of almost unlimited athletic facilities and equipment is included in the room rate of this laid-back establishment.

Afterwards, stroll along the carriageway from Paradise Paradise, turning left at the Club Mediterranée entrance and following the path leading to the elegant **Paradise Island Casino**. There is round-the-clock action here, in a 'smaller' – 30,000sq feet (2,800sq m) – and more subtly decorated casino competitor of Carnival's Crystal Palace. Try your luck with the roulette wheel, or one-armed bandits that accept anything from 5-cent pieces to $100 coins.

But you shouldn't linger here if you want to catch the magical Cloisters Garden before dusk. Leaving by the casino's main entrance, turn right, and walk in the direction of the Paradise Island Bridge. A few hundred yards along, turn left on to Paradise Island Drive (by the street sign). The walk along the dual carriageway is about 15 minutes, and is a pleasant stroll past the Comfort Suites, an exclusive time-share resort at the corner of Paradise Island Drive.

The **Cloisters** are the remains of a 14th-century French stone monastery imported to the United States by newspaper baron William Randolph Hearst in the 1920s. Forty years later, grocery-chain heir Huntington Hartford bought them and had them installed at the top of a hill overlooking Nassau Harbour. They have become a popular venue for weddings; a couple may organise a ceremony through the Ministry of Tourism's People-to-People programme, with a Bahamian minister officiating. Tasteful arrangements can be made for a simple and romantic outdoor ceremony.

The Cloisters: an import from 14th-century France

Cold embrace in the Versailles Garden

The **Versailles Garden**, also the creation of Hartford, is located between the Cloisters and the posh Ocean Club. It is a formal garden, terraced into seven levels, with a number of marble and bronze statues.

Watching the sunset while walking back over the 70-ft (20-m) high, 1,700-ft (520-m) long arching **Paradise Island Bridge** is a magical experience. Should you prefer some local colour, hop on board the jitney at the end of the bridge, once you've reached the Nassau side. Bus-stops on New Providence are sometimes marked, as at the area at the end of the bridge, but often just an upraised arm will get the driver's attention. And don't worry about causing a distraction any time your arm is raised; these drivers can distinguish a customer from someone waving to someone else. Located in front of the small shopping plaza, the jitney will take you back downtown. The cost is 75 cents; make sure you have the exact change. The bus will stop near the Best Western British Colonial Hotel, at the western end of Nassau's shopping mile. Here you should get off the first bus, and on to one marked 'Cable Beach', the Bahamian Riviera. (You'll have to pay again.) The beach is a direct route along Bay Street, with a scenic drive along the coastline which takes about 15 minutes (10 minutes by cab). There is also a free express shuttle service between Cable Beach and Paradise Island every hour; it stops at the lobby entrances of all major hotels.

You should ask to stop at **Carnival's Crystal Palace.** At 35,000sq feet (3,250sq m), this is the largest casino in the Caribbean. It has 750 slot machines, 60 blackjack tables, 11 craps tables, American and European roulette, baccarat, and other interesting ways to 'lose your shirt' – including horseracing – on a table! Here the Galactica Suite, complete with its own robot attendant, used to be let for $25,000 a night. Now it is offered on a complimentary basis to high rollers and VIPs. Guided tours of the Galactica are available.

In the casino, you can experiment with everything from a 5-cent one-armed bandit to the more pricey baccarat tables. And if you don't know what you are doing but want to learn, the casinos on Paradise Island and Cable Beach provide free gaming lessons, with complimentary cocktails.

Top off the evening with the Las Vegas-style revue at the Crystal Palace's **Jubilation** supper club.

A matter of luck

Excursions through the most popular attractions on New Providence, to the west of downtown Nassau. See map on page 24.

Start your morning early with an eggs and grits breakfast in the leisurely ambiance of **Coco's Cafe**, in downtown Nassau near the Sheraton Best Western British Colonial Hotel. If you prefer to have just a quick bite, right next door is Nassau's sole **Dunkin Donuts** outlet. Located across the street from the hotel, this is one of the oldest counter restaurants in Nassau, and is often used by the locals as a reference point for giving directions. The Cable Beach jitneys, whose route follows the shoreline towards the western part of the island, regularly stop at this spot, making the corner cafeteria the commuter's best friend. Breakfast muffins and coffee do a good business here, and service is no-frills but prompt.

You may have begun to feel a bit daunted by the apparent paucity of affordable restaurants in the city's urban centre. At this end of Bay Street, however, finding somewhere cheap to eat is not really a problem. Just three buildings away – two past Coco's – is a McDonald's, and two other fast-food outlets, Arby's and Wendy's,

are just around the bend of Bay Street, at the most western end of the Bay Street shopping mile. All of these serve breakfast, and many of them have Bahamianised a few items on their standard menu.

The Cable Beach jitneys will be visible when you walk out of any of these establishments. Hop on board, and ask the driver to let you off at the **Fisherman's Market**, located about five minutes' drive

Fisherman's Market

away. On the opposite side of West Bay Street from where you disembark will be a fruit and vegetable stand, at the corner of the side street called Chippingham Road. The vendors can help you identify some local fruits in season. You may see your first sugar-apple, sapodilla, guava, mango – or even tamarind and soursop. Guineps are plentiful, too; they look like a bunch of grapes with a tough green covering, but a bite through the hard outer shell releases a sweet juice. Be adventurous!

Behind the fruit stall is **Fort Charlotte**, one of 12 fortifications in the Nassau area. Built in 1789 by Lord Dunmore and named in honour of the wife of King George III, it has never fired a shot in battle. Local guides are available to show you the waterless moat, drawbridge, ramparts, and dungeons.

Just southwest of the fort are the **Botanical Gardens**, featuring more than 600 species of flowering trees and shrubs. There is a recreated Lucayan village in the grounds, and an impressive look-out point from where visitors can see everything – from the garden and village areas, to the hills and valleys of Centreville Nassau.

The **Ardastra Gardens and Zoo** is literally next door. It comprises 5 acres (2ha) of beautiful tropical gardens, complete with iguanas, monkeys, snakes, lizards, and birds, including the rare Bahamas parrot, and the world-famous marching flamingos. The more interesting trees are labelled with informative plaques. You'll also see Bahamian fruits growing in their natural habitat, and plants like mahogany, frangipani and cabbage palm.

Back at the Fisherman's Market create your own lunch from the selection of the fresh fruits and conch dishes, prepared while you wait. A sure giveaway that you are a tourist is the way you pronounce the name of this latter national staple. Be sure to call it 'conk', and see how quickly the vendors warm to you. The most popular raw versions of conch are in salad – made with chopped conch, onions, tomatoes, green pepper, and lime juice – and 'scorched conch' – where the conch meat is not burned, but tenderised with a meat hammer, and then plopped in a plastic bags, along with lemon juice and hot pepper sauce. There are no knives or forks for this snack – you just put your hand in the bag and tear off a piece of the meat. Conch is high-protein and low-calorie – a dieter's delight. The calories increase a bit if you eat whole conchs fried in batter ('cracked' conch), but the crispy batter and chewy consistency of the dish make it worth sampling.

Most stalls have eclectic decor and seating for their customers, so you can actually dine where you are. Fishermen also have available the day's catch, which is probably grouper, snapper, or crayfish

Birds of a feather (lobster). If you are near your hotel, it is not uncommon to buy something fresh like this and request the chef at your hotel to prepare it for you.

The market site also serves as the entrance to private vehicle access to Arawak Cay and Silver Cay, the man-made islands that house **Coral World** – a 16-acre (6-ha) underwater observatory and marine park. Its white observation tower is visible for miles from land or sea. Though there is a pedestrian and public access past the Fisherman's Market, it's almost a mile to walk and this option is probably best left to another day when you have more time. In the meantime you can call Coral World (328-1036). It provides a bus shuttle to and from most of the hotels, and offers a lovely ferry shuttle from Paradise Island.

The tower at Coral World

The tower is the focal point of Coral World. It descends 20 feet (6m) below sea level, and has a 360-degree glass-windowed room. The 8-foot (2-m) windows reveal a breathtaking view of live coral, sponges, tropical fish, and exotic marine life. There are also 24 marine garden aquariums here and an outdoor stingray pool. At the coral shop or the pearl bar you can buy hand-crafted jewellery. Choose a pearl-producing oyster and the pearl you find is yours to keep. In the pools you can pet a starfish or watch a shark feeding, as you explore the underwater without getting (totally) wet. Not to be missed is the **Tower Bar**, which serves devastating Daiquiris along with the great view.

If you'd rather walk back to the downtown area from the market, you should allow an hour or so. If it's a Friday or Saturday, you'll probably see a cricket match in progress at the famed **Haynes Cricket Oval**, on the sloping green just below the fort.

On the opposite side of Bay Street, facing the water, is a raised open space called the **Western Esplanade**. It actually runs into the fish and vegetable markets at its far end, at the junction of West Bay Street and Chippingham Road. Though it just looks like a patch of green during a weekday, on any – and almost every – weekend afternoon, locals pitch tents, fire up the charcoal, and have 'cook-outs' here. Fish, chicken, conch, and spare ribs are prepared the way Bahamians like – a bit spicier than the watered-down restaurant fare – and full meals are sold in styrofoam containers for a few dollars a plate. If you've managed a weekend visit to Nassau, try to get to one of these events. It's a great way to see the locals when they're not dressed to impress for Bay Street. Besides,

Feeding the stingrays at Coral World

Bungee jumping

the food is always best when you know the chef will eat it!

Continuing your walk back to town, you might want to try the 110-foot (33-m), New Zealand-style **bungee jumping** ride, which is available to daredevils from early morning till after sunset. A cage is suspended more than 100 feet (30m) above Nassau harbour, with cruise ships supplying both the background and the witnesses, as you free-fall towards the aquamarine water. The glorified rubber band wrapped around your ankles slows your fall before you make the big splash, and then twangs you back up, to fall again. The New Zealanders who run the bungee boast they have had 150,000 jumps without an accident.

For the less brave but equally adventurous, the next stop on your walk is **Marlborough Antiques**. It has one of the world's best collections of early photos of the Bahamas. Antiques, too, of course, as well as an interesting selection of books, jewellery, writing paper, and works of local Bahamian artists. A co-owner, Brent Malone, is a distinguished artist in his own right, whose oil-on-canvas 'junkanoo' scenes portraying Caribbean parades, grace many an international collection.

Now that you are back in downtown, you can visit more than a dozen art galleries and museums dotting Bay Street and its side-streets. A recent cultural rebirth stemming from quincentennial celebrations has created a new momentum within the artist community, as well as a more appreciative public. Fortunately for the tourist this means that many original works of art are both affordable and easy to carry home in your suitcase. Some of the more interesting ones are to be found among the bric-a-brac of the previously mentioned Straw Market (see *page 23*), but be sure you give yourself a good few hours to browse there.

For immediate 'just right' souvenirs, try **Charlotte's Gallery**, on Charlotte Street (just off Bay, and opposite the Straw Market). It promotes lesser-known as well as established Bahamian artists, whose junkanoo paintings, done in brilliant acrylics, may be the best kind of souvenir. On display are mini-lithographs, greetings cards, pottery, and even miniature pieces of stained-glass art. **Caripelago**, on East Street a few side-streets farther on, and **Best of the Bahamas**, near the intersection of Bay and Parliament streets, are fine examples of good small local galleries, with both arts and souvenirs.

Calypso till you can't

Heading towards the Woodes Rogers Walk, don't miss the chance to experience the sights and sounds of the cultural treasure known as junkanoo, at the multimedia **Junkanoo Expo**. Junkanoo paintings and handicrafts are on display and for sale in this converted customs warehouse on Prince George Wharf, and there is an impressive display of award-winning costume pieces from junkanoo competitions. A video presentation shows clips of past parades. There's nothing like being in the middle of thou-

sands during the junkanoo frenzy of Christmas and New Year on Bay Street; but if you're not able to be there during the season, this is the next best thing.

For your evening's entertainment you should head back out to Cable Beach. Hop the bus just around the corner from the Junkanoo Expo, at the piece of the road separating Arby's and the Best Western British Colonial Hotel, and you'll have a leisurely ride westward along Bay Street, towards the Cable Beach strip otherwise known as the 'Bahamian Riviera'. Cable Beach, incidentally, got its name from the transoceanic cable that extended from Nassau to just north of Palm Beach, Florida. Today the cable continues to provide the telephone link between the US and the Bahamas.

If you're not shopped out, try the massive indoor promenade that connects the **Crystal Palace Casino** with hotels at each end. there are exclusive dress and jewellery stores, duty-free liquor shops – everything from tobacco stores to hair salons. The prices reflect the locale, however, and are rather high. Either window-shop or come prepared to buy a Paris or Rome original.

Have your sunset dinner on the terrace of **Cafe Johnny Canoe**, next to the Nassau Beach Hotel. The decor is rustic, with brilliantly-coloured junkanoo art interspersed among

black-and-white photos of the Bahamas of yesteryear. This place serves the best broiled grouper on the island. A three-piece combo plays Bahamian rake'n'scrape, and a junkanoo group, replete in colourful costumes, 'rushes' through the restaurant, to the rhythm of the heated goatskin drums and cowbells.

The Nassau Beach Hotel's downstairs nightclub features the live music of the Bahamian legend King Eric and His Knights – complete with fire dancing, steel drums, and 'calypso till you can't'.

Serves the best boiled grouper

4. Around the Island

A long day's driving tour around the coastline of New Providence, taking in some smaller settlements and beachside bistros. Nighttime, the dancing is non-stop at Nassau's most popular local disco.

There are a dozen major hotels in the downtown area of Nassau. Each has mini-scooters available for rent. The scooter guides will provide you with a map, helmet, and a full tank of gas. That will be all you need – excluding your suntan lotion and camera, of course – as you follow this itinerary to tour the island of New Providence at your leisure.

Before heading for the outskirts, there are some historical sites you won't want to miss. Park your scooter near the **Main Post Office** in East Street, and visit some of them. A few minutes from this part of the city centre is an interesting collection of history. Located off Shirley Street on Elizabeth Avenue, are the 65 steps of the **Queen's Staircase**, each representing a year of Victoria's reign. Carved out of solid limestone by slaves in the 18th century, it was originally built to provide access from the town to the fort. At the top is **Fort Fincastle**, shaped like a paddlewheel steamer. Built in 1793 by Lord Dunmore,

The Queen's Staircase

this fort boasts a spectacular view from its lighthouse. Beside it is the **Water Tower.** Built in 1928, the tower still maintains the city's water pressure, and at 216 ft (65m) above sea level, it is the island's highest point. A lift takes you to the observation deck for a panoramic view of New Providence.

Now you're ready to return to your scooter and move out of the city. Go west along Bay Street, past Dunkin Donuts and Marlborough Antiques. As you drive away from the downtown area, the shoreline will always be on your right. Passing stately mansions of 19th-century architecture, you'll see the striking and multicoloured **Carnival's Crystal Palace** complex across the water. If you've been following the itineraries above you'll have discovered this place al-

Carnival Crystal Palace

ready, but this is a building that never fails to provoke a strong personal reaction. It has been described as everything from beautiful to horrendous, but I'll leave you to make up your own mind.

Continuing west, you will see a **golf course** on your left. Built in 1929 by Robert Trent, Jr., it is a popular par 72, 18-hole course. On the right side of the dual carriageway, at the roundabout, is **Goodman's Bay**, the unofficial entrance to the Cable Beach area, and itself a public beach. Power walkers and joggers are common here, and the spot is very popular with the aerobics set.

This section of the island is ideal for walkers. Small footpaths have been etched into the promenade which separates West Bay Street's east and west traffic flow. Ample shade is provided by arching casuarina trees, and pedestrians can walk for miles without worrying about the hazards of traffic.

Continue on, past the Cable Beach casino strip, stopping at **Stephania's Capriccio Cafe** for some homemade ice cream. Located at the Swanks' roundabout, this tiny cafe-cum-delicatessen also makes several different kinds of pasta. The owner, Stephania, personally tests each batch before serving it to her customers. The success of this little place, situated among a chain of major hotel complexes and private villas, attests to its simple ambiance and authentic Italian flavour.

Another two miles, and you're at **Delaporte Point**, which has its own beach. Here you can take a few minutes to hop off the scooter and on to a jet ski to fly along miles of uncluttered beach while getting a

Wave runners

closeup of the many sailboats and windsurfers. Parasailing is also available here: a nylon parachute-like sail is hooked to a boat that pulls you aloft and zooms around while you get a bird's-eye view of the island.

The **Caves** are a further two miles along Bay Street. Developed naturally out of soft limestone, they have the arrival of Prince Alfred of England in 1861 inscribed on their walls. Not far away, on the left side, is Blake Road, which leads into John F. Kennedy Drive and the **Nassau International Airport**. When the current $60 million expansion project is completed, this airport will have the largest and best-equipped customs and immigration pre-clearance facilities in the region.

But stay on Bay Street, because **Gambier Village** is just around the bend. The village was originally settled by liberated Africans after the abolition of slavery in 1807, and descendants of the oldest settlers of the island live here.

Seagrape Boutique

Traveller's Rest will probably tempt you to stop for a bit. Only about 10 minutes from the Crystal Palace, the relaxed, island-flavoured restaurant and bar is a favourite watering-hole. It is said that every once in a while, every Nassuvian makes their way here Androsian print tablecloths, local artwork, and murals festoon the walls. You'll probably see some patrons playing backgammon or Connect Four at one of the tables on the terrace. Adjoining the Rest is the charming **Seagrape Boutique**, which sells everything from Androsia fashions to handpainted jewellery and T-shirts. Browse through, and get that extra tube of sunscreen that you probably need by now.

Minutes away is the world-famous **Compass Point Studios**, used by the likes of Mick Jagger and Julio Iglesias. On either side of the winding road are the private estates of some of the more well-to-do inhabitants of the island. Between here and the next residential area, extending for about a quarter-mile (½km) along the shore, is **Love Beach**, a popular picnic spot for locals.

Contrast this with the next residential area, **Lyford Cay**, where your neighbours – if you've got a few million – are Sean Connery and Arthur Hailey. Princess Diana and Nelson Mandela are among the occasional guests who come to indulge in this exclusive enclave's luxury country-club atmosphere. At the entrance is a gate guarded 24 hours a day, so unless you have a special invitation, don't try to get in. You can, however, browse through the small shopping centre located just outside the security gates.

Now leave the shopping centre, go around the roundabout and up the hill. You'll be passing a few residential areas, including **Mount Pleasant**, which was once the living quarters for the Lyford Cay service staff, but is now a middle-class suburb for Bahamians of all professions. **Clifton Point** occupies a sharp curve which veers to the left, indicating that you have reached the westernmost tip of the island. As you continue past here, you'll notice the Clifton Pier Power Station on the left-hand side. This provides electricity for the entire western end of New Providence Island.

It is at this point that Bay Street finally changes to Southwest Road. As you continue your drive, you'll see the

A chance to push the boat out

West Bay St Beach

Ramada South Ocean Beach, one of the newer resorts on the island. Stop in and get yourself a cool Bahama Mama to quench your thirst. As you resume the tour, the road will continue on to become Adelaide Road. Although the road changes its name you shouldn't worry about getting lost: you're always on the same major route. Don't be tempted to meander down any of the unmarked side-streets (most lead to residential areas).

A signpost announces the historical **Adelaide Village** turnoff on your right, but keep on going; the ruins of historic slave huts are in this area, but are hard to find, even for the locals. If you'd like more information, call the **Bahamas National Trust** (393-1317), a non-profit organisation responsible for the preservation of Bahamian places of historic interest and natural beauty.

Continue along the Adelaide Road until it becomes Carmichael Road after you go through the roundabout at **Coral Harbour**. This is where the Bahamas Defence Force – the Bahamian version of the Canadian Mounties and the US Marines, all in one – have their main base.

Go through this intersection, continuing straight on Carmichael Road. A few miles along there will be a sign on the right, announcing the entrance to the **Bacardi Rum Distillery**. This is worth the detour; turn right, and take a half hour or so to visit the property. There's a small building just inside the Bacardi grounds, with a bar where visitors can sample some of the different blends of the world-famous rum.

After the brief stop, go back to the Carmichael Road intersection and turn right. Keep on Carmichael Road until you reach the traffic light at the T-junction of Carmichael and **Blue Hill Road**. This is a fairly densely populated suburban area, with not much of historical note; but you do get an impression of middle-class Bahamian lifestyle here.

Bahamian building

Turn left at the T-junction on to Blue Hill Road, and then take the second right, which will put you on Soldier Road. The next set of traffic lights will indicate the intersection of Soldier and Robinson roads. Turn right at the light; the road now becomes Prince Charles Avenue.

Continue all the way along to the absolute end of the road. You are now at the eastern end of the island, called **McPherson's Bend**. Enjoy the scent of the sea as you continue along the shoreline for about 6 miles (9km). The drive along the shore is visually spectacular, as are the opulent homes of the upper middle class who live here.

By the time you reach Old Fort Beach, named simply **Montagu** by the locals, you've come three-quarters of the way around the island. This is the last open area before Paradise Island, and second only to the Western Esplanade (on West Bay Street) as the most popular local beach for 'cook-outs' – outdoor weekend public barbecues – with chicken, seafood dishes, and pastries on sale.

Here also is **Fort Montagu**, the oldest of the three forts on New Providence, built in 1741 from local limestone. You might want to try a dish of conch salad at the **Poop Deck**, the terrace bar overlooking Nassau Harbour. Or turn left at the Paradise Island roundabout a few hundred yards along, and then left again at the traffic light onto Shirley Street, to the **Main Street Cafeteria**. It serves an all-Bahamian menu, cafeteria-style, at affordable prices.

For the evening, try a serenade at the **Vintage Club**, in the Buena Vista Restaurant on Delancey Street, in the city centre. Live traditional and contemporary jazz are served up here, along with a sumptuous dinner. For something less sedate, drive out to the Western Esplanade towards Coral World. Turn left at the intersection of West Bay Street and Nassau Street. At the traffic light at the bottom of the hill is **Rosalee's Takeaway**, Nassau's best version of a 'greasy spoon'. For four or five dollars, you can get a cracked conch dinner or chicken-in-a-bag. All the food is fried, and all comes with French fries topped with a combination of catsup and hot sauce. The bag will ooze grease, but the flavour is superb!

At this point you might want to return to your hotel to relax a bit before the evening's activities. This time you should let someone else do the driving, and take a taxi to the **Family Island Lounge**, a local nightclub a bit off the main thoroughfare, and very popular with Nassuvians. A live band is in attendance, the atmosphere is informal, and the dancing non-stop.

Conch Salad

My own selection of the best half-day boat excursions to nearby islands and coral reefs.

Ready to get away from it all? Take the Getaway Cruise from the Calypso Dock, at Paradise Island, for a 35-minute scenic ride to **Blue Lagoon Island**. The triple-deck *M/V Calypso* drops you on this uninhabited island, site for several scenes from the movie *Splash*. Free snorkelling gear is provided, and volleyball and table tennis are as strenuous a sport as you might want, as you laze the day away. The nature trails are short, and the fauna and flora pretty.

If you've signed up for the educational 'Dolphin Encounter', you'll see an introductory video about dolphins, followed by a brief question-and-answer period, during which live dolphins (did you know they have *three* stomachs?) play around you as you stand in waist-deep water, or swim around your toes as you sit on a floating platform. Spend the afternoon enjoying your prepared picnic lunch after swimming or snorkelling the day away. *M/V Calypso* also has a 3-hour dinner cruise, with a live band for dancing before and after the dinner of beef and fresh seafood.

Alternatively, get the **Beach Runners** to collect you from your hotel and carry you away on a scarab powerboat for a full- or half-day island-hopping exploration of 'remote sites on nearby islands.' Barbecued lunch and full open bar are included in the charter, which holds up to 15 people.

Alternatively you might want to consider Nassau's only underwater boat adventure: the **Atlantis Submarine**. A state-of-the-art, 28-seat, 50-ton submarine descends to depths of up to 150 feet (45m) below the ocean's surface. The adventure includes a round-trip ticket and history of the island in an air-conditioned bus. Passengers are taken to a white sand beach off West Bay Street, near Lyford Cay, and then by ferry to the submarine. They then have an hour's look at the seafloor on the *Atlantis*, complete with expert narration and identification of Bahamas marine life. The coral is magnificent. There's a free shuttle service to the Atlantis office from the major hotels.

For a glass-bottom boat ride, check out **Booze and Cruise Co. Ltd**, whose *Lucayan Queen* allows you to see underwater ship-

Dolphin encounters

A 'Booze and Cruise' boat

wrecks and a Bahama sea garden. On-board entertainment includes a limbo-dancing contest, and the price of the trip covers unlimited cocktails and delicious snacks. The *Lucayan Queen* departs from the Paradise Island Dock at 1pm (it organises a bus pick-up from Cable Beach) and returns at about 5pm (Tel: 393-3722).

Afterwards, indulge in a homemade pizza or burger at **Ed and Mario's**, a restaurant-bar on West Bay Street featuring, gratis, their unique video trivia game at your table; you can win prizes while playing trivia against other competitors both inside the restaurant and abroad in the US and Canada.

6. Excursion to Exuma

Powerboat for a day to a naturalist's dream island. From coral reefs to feeding iguanas, this is eco-tourism at its best.

Just 38 miles southwest of Nassau, the Exumas make up a 120-mile (190-km) long archipelago. With a base of craggy rock, the beaches are quiet, clean and seldom see what you might call a crowd. And with more than 360 cays, they have the reputation of being the most unspoilt and secluded of all the Bahama Islands.

The Exumas are most well-known to the sailing set, who cruise there regularly for the annual Family Island Regatta. The closest thing you can find resembling population density is Great Exuma Island, at the farthest end of the Exuma chain, with a total of about 2,000 residents.

The next – and some say most – exciting spectator sport is the action happening below the surface. Take a 900-horsepower boat from Nassau Harbour to the fabulous Exuma Cays for the day. The **Powerboat Excursion** to Exuma leaves from the Captain Nemo Dock (off Bay Street) in downtown Nassau at 9am. Each trip only takes six to eight couples, so make your reservations as soon as you get to your hotel (Tel: 327-5385).

With a motor that's four times more powerful than a standard V8, it should come as no surprise that you'll find you have reached the Cays in an hour.

There are scheduled stops along the way that remind you there's a whole world under the water you might have forgotten while you were at the casino. The Exumas are a protected Bahamas marine Park and a National Trust Reserve. That translates into few people and plenty of marine life. The waters fairly teem with snapper, grouper, and lobster, and with more corals than you can imagine.

At **Allan's Cay**, you'll see 3-ft (1-m) long iguana wiggling through the bush. The guides give an interesting talk about them, afterwards serving a mid-morning snack of fresh fruit. You'll probably end up giving most of yours to the iguanas, who are partial to green grapes and rush to the shoreline whenever they see the powerboat approaching. The second stop is made at a spectacular reef in crystal clear water, with many fish and coral formations. Even a timid swimmer will find a shallow swim other-worldly; the underwater shoals are positively stunning.

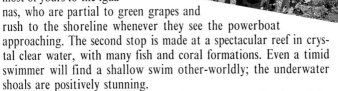

On the guided nature walk, you'll get a panoramic view of the island and learn some mysteries of the Bahamian bush. You'll see ospreys and egrets – maybe even a wild boar. Halfway along the walk, you'll be doused at the freshwater well. You can safely feed stingrays while ankle-deep in a pool of them. And provided the tide is right, the captain will hand-feed small sharks and barracuda while you stand by and watch.

Lunch will be barbecued lemon grouper on the beach at **Ship Channel Cay**. There are free refreshments all day long, from water and juice to wine and local Kalik beer. The beaches are private and the snorkelling spectacular. There's shelter, shade, and a rinse-down shower and toilet facilities.

After lunch, there's more island exploring or, if you prefer more leisurely pursuits after an energetic morning you can simply do some gentle working on your tan for the rest of the afternoon.

By 7pm, the boat is back at the Nassau dock.

Feeding the iguanas

Eleuthera
The Family Islands

There is no public transport on the Family Islands. Tourists make their way by either rental car or tour guide. The latter is rare, as most Family Islanders have full-time farming or fishing commitments. Rental cars are accessible but not plentiful, so they should be reserved in advance by your travel agent. Driving is done with cars keeping to the left side of the road. (As the Bahamian saying goes, 'If you're left, you're right; if you're right, you're wrong.')

There is only one major paved road on Eleuthera, called the Queen's Highway, which makes it practically impossible to get lost, even as a tourist. Most side-roads are unmarked, and have always been so. The narrow paths often compete with overgrowth, dirt, and loose rock, and only the sturdiest jeeps can brave some of them. Never mind; tucked behind almost every craggy limestone cliff are smooth, tranquil, pink-sand hideaways well worth seeking out.

Long and narrow in shape, Eleuthera is 110 miles (180km) of gently rolling hills from end to end, and 2 miles (3km) across at its widest point. The narrowest part of the island is at the Glass Window Bridge, which is only large enough to permit one car at a time to pass. Some settlements have pay phones, but you can be assured of phone access at every settlement's telecommunications station. The electricity in all areas is quite reliable. The tap water – unlike that of New Providence — is delicious. There are medical clinics in Governor's Harbour, Rock Sound, and Harbour Island, and a nurse's station in the smaller settlements.

Every which way

Hitchhiking short distances is a common practice by locals and foreigners alike, and is safe. On the whole, Family Islanders are extremely sociable; it is rare for them to lock their doors at night, and walking or driving, they are sure to hail friend or newcomer with a wave and a 'Mornin'!'

Preparing lunch

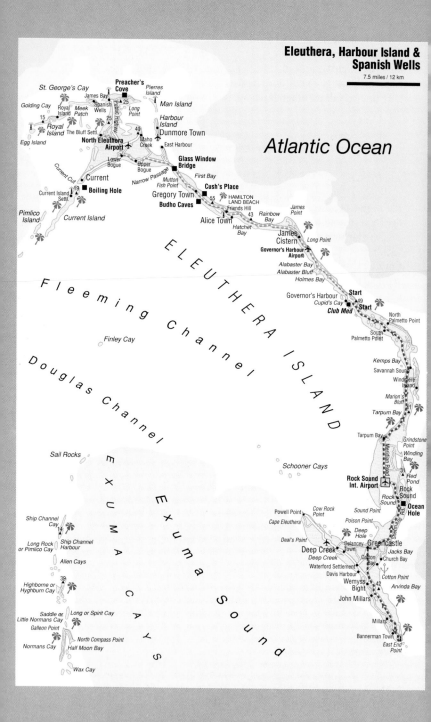

Visits to settlements in Central and South Eleuthera. The island's airport is near Governor's Harbour, the second-largest settlement on Eleuthera, and is half-an-hour's flying time away from Nassau. Visitors would do well to pick up a rental car at the airport on arrival, as other forms of transport are very limited.

View of Cupid's Cay

From the airport exit, turn right on to Queen's Highway, the one that covers the island from north to south. To start your day, you'll travel south, to **Governor's Harbour** itself. (I recommend you return here to stay the night: see the end of this itinerary for details of accommodation.)

'The Harbour', as it's called by the locals, has grown up around the picture-postcard **Cupid's Cay**. The colonial influence is still very strong here, as you'll see from the exquisite Victorian architecture displayed in well-maintained homes. These houses could easily belong to the early 19th century if they didn't seem in such good condition.

The 276-room **Club Mediteranée**, just around the corner and up the hill from the Harbour's one and only traffic light, was designed with the family in mind. Parents can pursue their own interests while children are supervised in land and water activities, including sailing, scuba-diving and even swinging from a giant trapeze. The Club also offers non-guests lunch or an evening cabaret show in the outdoor amphitheatre.

Then it's on down the Queen's Highway, for a tour of the south. The road passes through Palmetto Point, and a few miles farther on, Savannah Sound. In the neighbourhood is **Club Eleuthera**, an Italian-owned, smaller version of the French Club Mediterranée. It has a mostly Italian clientele with a very European atmosphere.

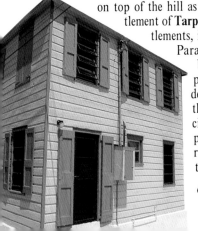

There's a real castle, owned by artist MacMillan Hughes, on top of the hill as you pass through the next settlement of **Tarpum Bay**. One of the prettiest settlements, it has a growing artists' colony. Paradise Sam Productions, on the bayfront, has T-shirts hand-painted and designed by a resident artist, Dorman Stubbs, and the Mal Flanders Studio specialises in inexpensive local scenes painted on driftwood. After Hurricane Andrew cut a swath through the island in the sum-

Colour counts in Tarpum Bay

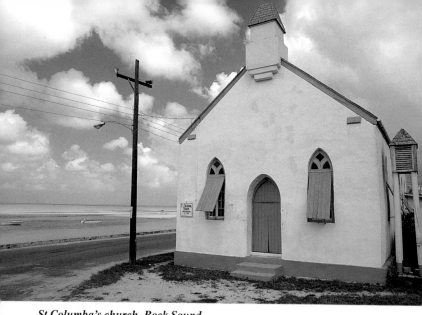

St Columba's church, Rock Sound

mer of 1992, Mal Flanders fashioned a Columbus scene out of the remains of the trunks of two coconut palms, and placed it in the yard between his home and studio. For very local nightlife, how could you resist a club here that's called The Dark End Of The Street?

A few miles farther along is **Rock Sound**, the largest settlement, which has an airport, and operates the main power station for the island. Get a local to point you in the direction of Nellie Lowe's Haven Restaurant and Pastry Shop. Nellie will fortify you with some decadent homemade pastries and cool refreshments. Grandma's Goodies, a shop near Nellie's bakery, sells great ice-cream if that's more your preference.

Five hundred yards further, on the right side of the road, is the **Ocean Hole**. If you have any to spare, you could share some of your ice-cream or pastry crumbs with the grouper and snapper fish that congregate at this pool, which is over 200 feet (60m) deep. The fish feed regularly from snacks thrown by tourists.

Continue along the highway, past Green Castle and Wemyss Bight, to **Davis Harbour** – a tiny marina where the island branches in two directions. If you turn right you can drive to **Deep Creek** and **Cape Eleuthera**, where a multi-million dollar resort is due to be completed soon. If you turn left, less than 20 miles (30km) away is **Bannerman Town**, at the end of the island. Its newest cay, man-made, is **Princess Cay**, which has a sprawling beach to

Weaving Straw

accommodate cruise ship passengers shuttled by boat to shore. At the dock is a mini-market which sells straw-work and junkanoo craft.

Now that you've seen the south I recommend you return to the centre and Governor's Harbour – a straight drive of about an hour. Here I'd recommend a couple of guest houses: either the small and accommodating **Carmen and Richard's Guest House**, or the beautifully landscaped **Laughing Bird Apartments**. Both are located near the centre of the settlement. In nearby Tarpum Bay is the **Unique Village**, with rooms and villas styled in white wicker and wood, and **Hilton's Haven**, located off the Tarpum Bay beach, for those on lower budgets.

In the evening you can shoot a game of billiards in the **Blue Room**, complete with a traditional chicken snack while you're serenaded by the old-fashioned jukebox. For something a little glitzier you can get seats for the Vegas-type show at Club Med. Or try **Ronnie's Hideaway**, on Cupid's Cay, just over the little bridge at Governor's Harbour. It's the 'in' local disco, with a live band every weekend. The country's biggest bands always have this club on their itinerary when they are on national tours.

The Eleuthera Ministry of Tourism representative has an office in Governor's Harbour, in the same building as the local post office. It will be well worth your while to take a few minutes to drop in for a chat; she'll let you know about all local events and festivals taking place during your stay on the island.

8. North Eleuthera

A driving tour from Central to North Eleuthera, from underground caves to pineapple plantations. The Glass Window Bridge and constellations by moonlight. See map on page 44.

Leaving Governor's Harbour

Check out of your Governor's Harbour hotel; you'll be moving to the northern end of the island today. Moving north on the Queen's Highway, away from Governor's Harbour, you'll pass through the 'Speed Bump Settlement' (there are 10 bumps in a row!) of **James Cistern**. Pull out your camera now; the **Cliffs**, just outside this settlement, provide a beautiful photo opportunity.

From one settlement's outskirts to the next, this is all open farm acreage. Eleutherans were once heavily into fruit and vegetable farming, until the lucrative shellfish industry lured them to sea. The island's settlements house a few hundred people at most, and many of the larger homes you see among the hills while driving along the highway belong to win-

47

Hatchet Bay Caves

ter residents. **Rainbow Bay** is an excellent example of this. The area's most popular restaurant is located at the **Rainbow Inn**, which rents out octagon-shaped wooden villas built on stilts. It has its own beach, which is great for picnics. The artwork and nautical souvenirs festooning the walls of its restaurant/bar are evidence of its popularity with yachtsmen who frequent it for its homey ambiance and marvellous evening's dining.

About ten minutes' drive away is the sign welcoming you to **Hatchet Bay**. Its busy, well-protected harbour draws many from the sailing set, and it also serves as a port for the government mailboat, which drops off passengers and supplies twice a week. After the sign, and just beyond the basketball court bordering the Queen's Highway on the left side of the road, is the turnoff to both the dock and the tiny settlement of **Alice Town**.

The **Hatchet Bay Caves** are about 3 miles (5km) farther along the highway. Replete with hundreds of leaf-nosed bats, they are a naturalist's dream. If you're interested, you can arrange for a local guide to take you through. (Ask while you're in Hatchet Bay.) You'll also need to ask directions to **Surfers' Beach**. About 3 miles (5km) past the caves, this beach is on the right, about a quarter-mile (½km) walk in from the highway, along somewhat rocky tyre treads. Park the car by the side of the road, and make the hike. After 15 minutes or so across what seems to be nothing but bush, a breathtaking expanse of beach appears over the crest of a small hill. Experts declare this is among the 10 best surfing beaches in the world. Even if you don't indulge in the sport, the majesty of those cresting waves is awe-inspiring.

Seven miles (12km) farther, past grain silos and open fields, is **Gregory Town**. Its 500 residents deserve the reputation of making it the friendliest settlement in the country. On the right side of the highway, just before the final hill leading into the settlement, is **Cush's Place**, the ideal spot for a cool drink and a friendly game of pool with the locals.

I recommend that you stay here, ideally at the hotel at

Surfers' Beach

Cambridge Villas. Once you've checked in, go straight to the restaurant and order their extraordinary conch chowder, served with decadently delicious homemade bread. The portions are big here, and when it comes to taste, the meals are definitely worth the wait. You may be surprised to order a hamburger, in this far-flung location, and find it to be the biggest, beefiest, and juiciest you've tasted in a long time. They also have first-rate fish-burgers, straight from the day's catch.

This region is pineapple country, with more than a hundred tons a year shipped to local markets in Freeport and Nassau. In 1844, Eleuthera sent its first shipment of pineapples to England. Eleutherans will tell you it was pineapple seeds gathered from the fields of Gregory Town that were first planted in Hawaii. The rest, shall we say, is history.

Stop in at the **grocery store**, and get some gas. You may also want to take home some world-famous Thompson Brothers pineapple rum, made from a closely guarded Gregory Town family recipe. Place your request at the store.

Ask anyone in the settlement for directions to the **Thompson Bakery**. At the top of the hill overlooking the settlement, the Thomp-son sisters have a little shop at the back of their home that specialises in mouth-watering pineapple treats. Sample their pineapple or coconut tarts. Their additive-free raisin bread is sold out daily; it's the kind you'll want to eat by the handful, without using butter or spreads. What the shop lacks in frills, it more than makes up for in personalised service.

Before you move on, visit the **Island Made Gift Shop**. Everything here is as it says, locally

Great gifts in Gregory Town

made, from jams to T-shirts and jewellery. And while you are here, get instructions about the turnoff to Gaulding Cay, your next stop.

Two miles (3km) past Gregory Town, make the turnoff at the left side of the road. **Gaulding Cay Beach** is an exquisite little stretch of beach, no more than a few hundred yards long tucked away at the end of the path. The water is shallow enough to wade out almost a quarter mile before it reaches hip level. And this in calm, emerald water so transparent that you can see the white sand of the sea floor and every little fish that moves.

Brush the sand from your toes, return to your car and move on to the most breathtaking natural spot on the island, just a few miles away. Park at the side of the road, and walk up on the **Glass Window Bridge**. It's not made of glass, but is an actual bridge one car-width wide which joins two pieces of the island at its narrowest

Glass Window Bridge

point. Far below, on one side of the bridge, are the crashing dark blue waves of the Atlantic. On the other, the emerald green sea is glassy-smooth, and hence the name.

About 15 minutes' drive away are **Upper** and **Lower Bogue**. Have a meal of minced lobster at the **Seven Seas Restaurant** before you cruise back to Gregory Town. You might want to go to Lower Bogue's **Purple May Club**, which has a live band every weekend.

For dancing till dawn, though, nothing comes close to the energy of a weekend disco at the **Cambridge Villas** back in Gregory Town. This is particularly true on a Friday night when the government mailboat makes the five-hour passage into Hatchet Bay from Nassau, usually loaded with Eleutherans returning from business in 'town' and adventurous tourists who probably missed the last flight to the island. On such evenings dinner is served from 6 to 8pm at the Villas. Then the tables in the centre of the dining-room are moved against the walls, the lights are turned down, and the disc jockey gets down to business. The dinner crowd slowly disappears into the dark, and evening revellers start to trickle in.

By midnight the mood shifts abruptly. The mailboat has docked, and its passengers are being shuttled to Gregory Town. They arrive at the Villas en masse. The lights are turned off; pop tunes are replaced with Trinidad *soca*, Bahamian rake'n' scrape, and Jamaican reggae, and the dance floor is packed within the space of a half hour. Even with the air conditioning going full-blast, you'll leave dripping with sweat, and feeling positively invigorated.

The most incredible memory you'll have of Eleuthera comes free of charge almost any evening: the sky. These islands have few cars and less industry. Due to low latitude, the Bahamas is probably the only place where you can see the southern hemisphere, and on a clear night the city-dweller may be shocked by the number of stars. I've been in Gregory Town during an evening power failure; even with all the street lights extinguished, there was enough starlight for pedestrians to make their way around. So bring along a guidebook to the constellations, and spend an evening with the stars!

A water taxi takes you to this tiny island off Eleuthera. No cars – just bicycles and golf carts – and a shopping district of pristine pink colonial cottages exuding. See map on page 44.

Harbour Island, just 3 miles (5km) long and half-a-mile (1km) wide, is five minutes by water taxi off the northern coast of Eleuthera. The well-maintained former Loyalist colony is famed for its 3-mile (5-km) wide pink sand beach. (The tiny grains are actually white sand mixed with white coral algae.) The quaint architecture is reminiscent of New England, and down-home hospitality exudes from the residents of this former shipbuilding community turned winter resort of the rich and famous. Scooters, bicycles, and golf carts are for hire at several locations, and make a great way to discover the island. Sports fishing and water tours are to be had by the hour or by the half day.

Harbour Island view

Dunmore Town is to Harbour Island what Nassau is to New Providence: the pulse of the island. It is the home of the oldest Anglican church in the Bahamas, **St John's**, which was built in 1768. The **fig tree** by the government dock is the equivalent of the town meeting place. Vendors and cabanas decorate the area; if there is anything worth talking about, they say you can be sure to hear about it first from under the fig tree. A stone's throw away is **Picaroon Landing**, a restaurant that occasionally makes a warm soup from oranges and bananas, and serves it with freshly baked bread. On the harbourfront across from the straw market is the **Sugar Mill**, which has a good selection of ceramics, pottery, jewellery, straw-work, and T-shirts. **Flo's Pastries**, on Clarence Street, sells fresh brown, banana nut, coconut, raisin, and corn breads.

Get an ice-cream cone from **Adelaide's Snack Bar** as you stroll through the streets. Then enjoy a sumptuous lunch at **Valentine's Yacht Club** and Inn, at the heart of historic Dunmore Town. The club offers a free introductory lesson in scuba-diving in the pool.

Guides are available for dives to a sunken train wreck not far offshore.

Angela's Starfish Restaurant at the top of the hill has a panoramic view of the island, and **Sea Grapes Nightclub** is home to former in-house, now recording artists – the Funk Gang – who return regularly to perform when not on tour.

Atlantic spadefish

Typical clapboard home in Spanish Wells

10. Spanish Wells

A day's visit to the crawfish capital of the Bahamas. Rustic charm in a fisherman's hideaway. See map on page 44.

Five minutes by water taxi to the northwest of Eleuthera is **Spanish Wells**, the crawfish (Bahamian lobster) capital of the Bahamas. The Spanish discovered that the water from this island's wells was the sweetest water they had ever tasted.

Most young men here leave school after 10th grade to enter the lucrative spiny lobster fishing business. They can earn tens of thousands of dollars during the 7-month season, catching lobster and storing them in freezers aboard a Bahamian 'smack'. Per capita, they're the richest community in the Bahamas.

The clapboard houses found in Spanish Wells bear a strong resemblance to New England fishing villages, and the lilt in pronunciation harks back to the British dialect of centuries ago. And distinctive, too, is the blond-haired, blue-eyed physical presence of these white Bahamians.

Cars are not for hire, though you can get bicycles. Sportfishing guides can take you around Royal and Russell islands, and the **Spanish Wells Yacht Haven** has dive facilities. Or get yourself a paddleboat and take your time discovering your own island secrets.

Check out the tiny **Quilt Shop** in downtown Spanish Wells, where prices for these works of art range from $285 to $325. The **Spanish Wells Museum** opened in 1991. Inside are artefacts dating back to Columbus's arrival in 1492, and relics from the Puritan Eleutheran Adventurers of 1648.

Afterwards, drop into the **Langousta** for an island lunch made from the day's fresh catch, and hear the latest fish story from the locals.

Take a water-taxi

Grand Bahama

Only 65 miles (105km) off the coast of Florida, towards the northern end of the Bahamas, Grand Bahama takes its name from the Spanish 'gran bajamar' ('the great shallows'). One of the last settled of the islands of the Bahamas chain, it became permanently inhabited in the early 19th century. Easy money from blockade-running during the US Civil War caused an abrupt exodus in 1861. Only when industrialist Wallace Groves created the design for a planned 'second city' at a clearing in a pine forest near Hawksbill Creek was the island's potential rejuvenated. He signed a lease – called the Hawksbill Creek Agreement – in 1955, for 50,000 acres (20,00ha) of land, pro-

On the edge: West End, Grand Bahama

mising in exchange a deepwater harbour. He would pay for all government personnel employed in this free port area (thus the capital city's name), and reimburse the government for all other services.

And Grand Bahama hasn't looked back. In contrast to Nassau, the wide, clean streets of Freeport are uncluttered of both traffic and litter. Water, electricity, telephones, and television are well-maintained, and residents of the Freeport/Lucaya area in particular are sophisticated in both dress and lifestyle. With few local bars or corner shops, the physical layout of the island's urban centre discourages panhandlers or loafers.

Bahamasair has four flights daily to Freeport from Nassau. Taino Air flies three times a week between Freeport and North Eleuthera. TWA has three flights daily from West Palm Beach, and Laker Airlines has flights twice daily from Miami. Though you must commute by cab or tour bus from the airport to the Freeport/Lucaya area, once downtown, local buses, at $1 per passenger, run the length of the island until sunset. Though taxi tours are available, it is recommended you get your own hire car, with rates ranging between $65–85 per day. Bicycles also can be hired at $20 per day, and scooters at $40 per day.

Rand Nature Centre

11. Freeport – Lucaya

Casinos, nature gardens, the International Bazaar, Port Lucaya and attractions to the east side of Freeport. Finish this long day with a romantic dinner at Pier One.

I've started this itinerary from the airport on the basis that most people will be flying in and hiring a car. However, if you are already staying in downtown Freeport, you can easily pick up the route from breakfast at Mr Baker's.

From the **Freeport National Airport** your first exit will be a roundabout called Independence Circle. Remember always to keep to your left. You will be on a short strip of road called the Mall. A left at the gas station would take you onto East Settler's Way, and towards the **Rand Nature Centre**, home of the Bahamas National Trust. It has nature trails and a low-key Bahamian guide who explains the flora and fauna of the island.

But you're going to keep on the main road for now. Past the Civic Centre there are three Canadian-owned banks on the right side of the road, with the main **Post Office** just visible behind the Royal Bank. (Canadian banks hold 80 percent of all deposits in the Bahamas.)

The next set of traffic lights marks the intersection with Pioneer's Way, the centre of the city section. On the left, in a colonial pink

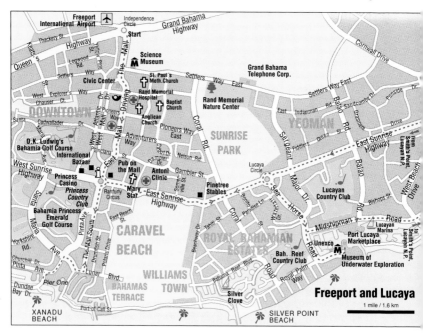

building, is the Grand Bahama Port Authority Headquarters. Grab a quick breakfast at **Mr Baker's**, which is across the road from Wendy's on East Mall Drive. Have them prepare a little box lunch for later on.

A mile or so further down the road – you're still on East Mall Drive – is Ranfurly Circus, named for a popular British colonial governor of the 1950s. It is the home of the famous **International Bazaar**, a collection of more than 90 shops, lounges, and restaurants with products and architecture representing almost 30 countries. At the entrance to the bazaar is a bright red, 35-ft (10-m) high *torii*, the Japanese traditional gate of welcome. Across the street is the **Winston Churchill Pub**, which offers bangers and mash (sausages and mashed potatoes) and a pint of British ale.

Hair care at the Bazaar

If you continue through the roundabout and along the Mall South, you will reach the **Princess Casino** and **Princess Country Club**. More than 500 rooms are arranged like the spokes of a wheel around a delightful plaza with hot tubs and swimming pool, completed by a waterfall. Adjacent is the John B, an open-air dining-room and bar, the perfect spot for a cool rum punch. Don't linger here – there is so much to see.

In the distance you can see the refinery and a deepwater harbour. On the channel entrance to that harbour is **Pier One**, built on stilts over the water like a New England fish warehouse. You can see the ships dock from here. Continuing straight down the mall, you'll get your first good view of the ocean.

Off Pier One is the **Xanadu Beach Resort**. Millionaire recluse Howard Hughes lived here for many years on its 12th and 13th floors, until his death in 1976. The Xanadu has a marina and there is another – the Running Mon – nearby.

But now go back to Ranfurly Circus, and turn right along the East Sunrise Highway. You will pass the Pub on the Mall, Pinetree Stables (trail and beach horseback trails), the Sunrise Shopping Centre (open after the downtown supermarkets are closed) and the Freeport High School.

Another mile along, just after the Coral Road intersection, you'll arrive at the Lu-

Upcoming attractions

The 'Dolphin Experience', UNEXCO

caya Circle. Three-quarters of the way around the circle takes you on to Sea Horse Road, which leads to the **Lucayan Beach**, home of the major hotels on the island. The **Lucayan Beach Hotel and Casino**, the first hotel on the island, is one of the busiest. Built as part of the conditions of the Hawksbill Creek Agreement, it was the first Bahamian hotel to have a casino when it opened in 1963. The multi-storey Atlantik Beach Hotel and casino is adjacent, and next door is the 526-room Holiday Inn.

The **Port Lucaya Marketplace** opened officially in 1989. With 85 Art Deco shops and ongoing open-air entertainment at the bandstand in Count Basie Square, it is probably the most popular spot on the island. To the north, across from the hotels, is an extensive, man-made canal system which has several small waterfront hotels and the largest yacht basin on the island: the **Lucayan Marina and Hotel**. A stone's throw away there are two more 18-hole golf courses: the original championship Lucayan Country Club, and the Bahama Reef and Country Club.

The Lucayan Beach area is where most of the action is. In the daytime there are organised boat trips for fishing and snorkelling. Next to Port Lucaya is the **Underwater Explorers Society** (UNEXCO). At UNEXCO, one of the most respected and comprehensive dive centres in the world, you can learn to dive, they promise, in just 3 hours. You can also swim with the dolphins, at their 'Dolphin Experience'. At Sanctuary Bay, probably the largest dolphin facility in the world, nine Atlantic bottlenose dolphins swim out to a reef to interact with scuba-divers in 40 feet (12m) of water. The less ambitious can mingle with them in an open water pool. You can parasail, too, or hire a Boston whaler or windsurfer. At night the Panache Club in the Holiday Inn gets busy.

Now return to the Lucaya Circle roundabout, and continue along the East Sunrise Highway. After about two miles, turn right at

Lucayan National Park Beach

Churchill Drive, then left on Midshipman Road. Get your camera ready; you're entering the **Garden of the Groves** – an exquisite 12 acres (5ha) of botanical gardens only 10 miles (16km) away from the city centre (about 15 minutes by car). Browse through the straw market at the entrance, and take a few minutes to visit the on-site **Grand Bahama Museum**, which contains marine life exhibits, an explanation of the African origins of junkanoo (the national festival), some junkanoo costumes, and rare artefacts of Lucayan Indians. The garden next door has 5,000 varieties of shrubs, trees and flowers. Wander through (and under) the waterfalls and ponds, and enjoy a visual feast to the eye of the exotic and brilliantly-coloured tropical plants, which seem to be springing up from everywhere.

From there, drive 15 miles (24km) farther east along Midshipman Road, to the **Lucayan National Park**. Signed trails will take you through a mangrove swamp, and the **Lucayan Caverns** – the world's largest underwater cave system. The sunlight playing on the water inside the caves is especially beautiful in the cooler early morning hours; snack on the goodies from your lunch box while you're there.

Then cruise back, along the wide, well-manicured and uncluttered East Sunrise Highway to the city centre. There should still be a few hours left of the day to wander around the shops at either **Port Lucaya** or the **International Bazaar** at Ranfurly Circus (both have tourist information offices). In the latter, take a tour of the **Perfume Factory**, where you can mix, bottle, name and label your own fragrance. Across the street, above Colombian Emeralds International, is another factory which you can also visit and watch local craftsmen create jewellery. If you don't feel like shopping, you can even take a paddleboat ride or a glass-bottom boat trip around the harbour.

Dine at **Pier One**, on a patio overlooking the shark show; they'll be feeding at the same time as you. A nice after-dinner touch at Pier One is the complimentary cognac for the men, and a glass of peach schnapps for the lady diners.

If you've opted for eating at Port Lucaya, there's a free native show here every night. You can stroll along the boardwalk stalls, or enjoy the live calypso and fire dancing under the stars till 11pm.

Dusk falls on Lucayan Beach

A tour of the western end of the island, rich in history and folk-lore, and a chance to perfect that suntan at any one of the beaches scattering the coast.

A tour of the West End may be the ideal way for you to take advantage of the Ministry of Tourism's 'People-to-People' programme. Begun in 1975, it has developed a scheme in which more than a thousand volunteers throughout the country are chosen, on the basis of age, interests, hobbies, and religious affiliations, to assist visitors at feeling 'at home away from home'. They give you a glimpse of Bahamian life as you might see it when visiting a friend – just as this book does. In advance, or even after you've landed on the island, you can call the People-to-People Unit of the Grand Bahama Tourist Office, located in the International Bazaar, at 352-8044.

Another option if you'd rather look than drive, is a bus tour from Freeport to Eight Mile Rock and West End. The 4-hour tours allow you to stroll through the streets, bargain at the local shops, and sample native dishes in the village restaurants. Check with the Tourist Information Centre or your hotel for more information.

With or without the company of a native, you can start the day with some coffee anytime after 7am at **Becky's**

Breakfast at Becky's

Restaurant, in Freeport's International Bazaar, located just in front of the *torii* gate. The basic American-style breakfast offerings of eggs and bacon or pancakes here is nothing to write home about; however, Becky's is one of the few non-hotel, centrally-located restaurants that open early in the morning, and the coffee is good, servers friendly, and more than happy to point out the right road for people needing good directions.

Not that the drive will be in any way daunting. Take the West Sunrise Highway to the Queen's Highway. A series of small settlements dots the route towards West End, at the far western tip of the island. Each place is small, with a few nondescript shops or

stores, but worth the look to appreciate the contrast between the Port Authority and the rest of the island. You should be careful as you drive, however: children play in the road day and night.

Rural region

Liquor store, Eight Mile Rock

Eight Mile Rock, the next settlement, is exactly that – stretching both east and west of the historical Hawksbill Creek. It is the Bahamas' third largest community after Nassau and Freeport. About 1 ½ miles (2km) into the Eight Mile Rock area, stop off and have a full breakfast at **Triple D Restaurant**. People in this area are very friendly. At **Hanna Hill**, about a mile away, it's quite common for tourists to walk about and chat with the folks from the community; locals will probably invite you to join them for a chat on their porch.

About a quarter mile farther along, you can stop for toiletries and a cool drink at the **Friendship Shopping Centre**. If the water is beginning to look tempting and you've brought along your swim gear, **Deadman's Reef**, near the small subdivision of Holmes Rock, has good diving off its cays. The Mount Olivet Baptist Church is the only point of interest in the Holmes' Rock and Seagrape area. Almost all of the residents of Seagrape are descendants of Turks and Caicos Islanders who first came to the island in the days before Freeport, when the lumber business was flourishing.

Just past Bootle Bay is the **Chicken Nest** – a local bar whose regulars will challenge you to a friendly game of pool or backgammon as Rosie, the proprietor, prepares a bowl of fresh conch salad that people make the 20-mile (30-km) drive from Freeport for.

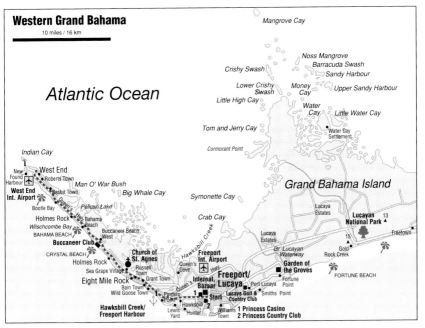

Western Grand Bahama

10 miles / 16 km

Atlantic Ocean

Mangrove Cay

Noss Mangrove
Barracuda Swash
Crishy Swash
Sandy Harbour
Lower Crishy Swash
Money Cay
Upper Sandy Harbour
Little High Cay
Water Cay
Little Water Cay
Tom and Jerry Cay
Water Cay Settlement
Cormorant Point

Grand Bahama Island

Indian Cay
New Found Harbour
West End
Roberts Town
Man O' War Bush
West End Int. Airport
Nesbit Town
Big Whale Cay
Symonette Cay
Lucaya Estates
Lucayan National Park 13
Bootle Bay
Pelican Lake
Crab Cay
Freetown
Holmes Rock
Bahama Beach
Wilschcombe Bay
Buccaneer Beach West
Lucaya Estates
BAHAMA BEACH
Gr. Lucayan Waterway
15
Gold Rock Creek
Buccaneer Club
CRYSTAL BEACH
Church of St. Agnes
Freeport Int. Airport
Garden of the Groves
FORTUNE BEACH
Holmes Rock
Russell Town
Queen's Cove
Sea Grape Village
Fortune Point
Eight Mile Rock
Grant Town
Internal. Bazaar
Freeport/ Lucaya
Smiths Point
Bain Town
Pinders
Port Lucaya
Wild Goose Town
Start
Lucaya Golf & Country Club
Hawksbill Creek/ Freeport Harbour
Lewis Yard
Hawksbill
Hunter
Williams Town
1 Princess Casino
2 Princess Country Club

Free rein on Russell Town Beach

West End, at the western tip of the island, has a main street lined with bars, shops, and houses. It was frequented by rum-runners and Al Capone during the bootlegging days of the US Prohibition. There is a service station and a straw market where you can purchase inexpensive last-minute souvenirs from this end of the island.

As you retrace your route to Freeport, take note of the turnoff to the right, at the entrance to the **Buccaneer Club**. It's the best restaurant on the island outside Freeport. Sprawling on to its own ¼-mile (½-km), pristine beach, it offers thatched cabanas on the outside patio, and provides a rustic ambiance indoors, with chandeliers and hurricane lamps above its spacious oak dining-room. It's the perfect place for your last evening's dining on the island, and worth the drive back from the city later on.

As you retrace your route, get a local to show you the '**boiling hole**' next to the coastal road along the ocean front of Eight Mile Rock. A boiling hole is an entrance to a subterranean cave system. A bubbling collection of water creates a vortex in both directions, depending on the tide, and the pressurised water coming out of the hole appears to 'boil'. Just past the Freeport Harbour, at **Pinders Point**, you'll see another 'boiling hole' called 'the chimney'.

Russell Town occupies a beautiful stretch of beach south of Freeport, at the southern end of North Beachway Drive, a road much used by equestrians from the **Pinetree Riding Stables**. Take a pleasant trail ride along their beach at this attractively landscaped, secluded spot.

If you are hunting beaches at the end of the day, there are others I'd recommend: just east of Lucaya, three fine beaches run into one another – Taino Beach, Smith's Point, and Fortune Beach. They

The end of another day

are popular with the locals as well as with tourists. Alternatively, take Midshipman Road past the Garden of the Groves to the Lucayan National Park, a 35-minute drive east of Freeport. You can spend a delightful few hours meandering through the honeycombed collection of limestone caves here. Across the road from the cave entrance, is a quiet, pristine white sand beach. It's the perfect place to take a break and work on your tan.

Then it's back to your hotel, with just enough time to change for dinner. Get a good seat for the casino show at the **Princess Casino** – a skilful and tasteful blend of native and Vegas-style entertainment.

Shopping

If you're interested in the exotic and the exclusive, you've come to the right place. Bay Street, the main street of downtown Nassau, is a shopper's paradise, carrying a 'who's who' of brand names of products from around the world. The same is true for the International Bazaar and the Port Lucaya Marketplace, on Grand Bahama.

The Bahamas government has recently eliminated the import duty on several international brand names. The Bahamas Duty-Free Promotion Board accredits merchants who give an unconditional guarantee of authenticity to every designer or brand name product they carry. Look for the pink flamingo symbol in the window of participating stores.

Don't expect to do much shopping when you get to Eleuthera or the other Family Islands. Clothing and gift stores are rare, the quality questionable, and the prices inflated. Once you're on any island other than New Providence or Grand Bahama, it's better to invest in the hospitality, good food, and clean beaches.

Bahamian-made Androsia fabric is a good find, as are the locally-made perfumes, liquors, and liqueurs. Visit the straw markets on any island, and try bartering with the vendors over the prices of shell craft, straw-work, and affordable local paintings. Conch, whelk and intricate coral and gold jewellery are also available. While sampling the local rums and liquors, you might want to try the national beer called Kalik.

Spoilt for choice

Leather

Prices for leather goods range from 15 to 40 percent less than in the United States. For everything from bags to shoes, be sure to visit the Brass and Leather Shop, on Charlotte Street in Nassau. The Fendi Boutique imports the real thing, direct from Italy. It's located at the corner of Bay and Charlotte streets in Nassau. And Gucci, located beside Rawson Square, has an excellent selection with a large range of accessories.

62

Crystal and China

Little Switzerland on Bay Street, Nassau, carries such lines as Waterford, Swarovski, and Lenox. The Midnight Sun in the International Bazaar in Freeport also has a varied selection, with such impressive names as Baccarat, Daum, and Herend.

Francis Peek, which is located on George Street in downtown Nassau, can boast that it offers one of the largest ranges of Herend hand-painted china in the western hemisphere.

Cameras and Clothing

John Bull's camera centre offers Nassau's finest display of cameras and photographic equipment. Nikon, Canon, Vivitar and Olympus cameras and related

Lalique glass on Bay Street

accessories are on sale at impressively discounted prices. They have several branches in Nassau, Paradise Island, and Freeport.

The pre-shrunk colourfast cotton fabric known as Androsia is batik-dyed, cut and sewn at the Androsia factory in Fresh Creek, Andros. Native fish, shells, flowers and birds are brilliantly displayed in such colours as conch pink, sea green, and aquatide. Look for it at the Mademoiselle shop, on Bay Street in Nassau, and in the Paradise Island Resort and Casino. It makes a distinctive gift to take home that has the advantage of being easy to squeeze into a suitcase.

Paradise Tees on Paradise Island is the exclusive distributor of the popular Panama Jack T-shirts.

Androsia batik is hard to resist

Local coral and pearl

Watches and Jewellery

The top merchant on Grand Bahama for both jewellery and watches is Colombian Emeralds International, the leading emerald retailer in the world, with major stores in both the International Bazaar, Port Lucaya Marketplace, and Princess Towers. Savings over US prices range from 20 to 50 percent.

The Tick-Tock Shop on Bay and Market streets, opposite the Straw Market in Nassau, has a wide array of unique, trend-setting timepieces. Look for the French design of the perennial favourite Mickey Mouse watch.

Paradise Jewels, in the Paradise Towers Casino on Paradise Island, has some semi-precious stones such as topaz, at 10 percent off the regular price.

Cartier's exclusive boutique on Bay Street carries a wide range of high-quality products. In addition to the renowned 18K gold Cartier jewellery, it sells sunglasses, watches, scarves, money clips, and letter openers – all bearing the Cartier name.

John Bull offers a wide array of quality merchandise, from watches and jewellery (Dolphin line, by Kabana, in 14K gold and silver) to perfume and cameras. Their exclusive watch lines include Rolex, Cartier, Gucci. John Bull also has certified Rolex technicians, and branches throughout both Grand Bahama and New Providence. The Paradise Island branch is open from 10am to midnight.

Gold and Diamonds has silver scales, pieces of eight coins, and gold doubloons, as well as ancient Greek and Roman coins. More than 1,500 gold items are manufactured locally from pure gold bullion, and all jewellery is duty-free. Visit their showroom on Bay Street, opposite the Straw Market.

Galleries

Junkanoo paintings commit to canvas the vivid Caribbean parades. A cluster of galleries situated around Bay Street in Nassau – try Charlotte's Gallery, Caripelago and Best of the Bahamas – are excellent sources of genuine local colour.

Perfumes

The Beauty Spot, on Bay Street, offers a complete line of American and French cosmetics, including Elizabeth Arden, Clinique, Estée Lauder, Lancombe, and Chanel.

Freeport's Caribe fragrance factory creates unique fragrances from special formulas, using native flowers like jasmine, frangi-

Works by local artists

Take home the taste of Kalik beer

pani, white ginger, gardenia, and fruits and herbs like bay rhum, lyme, spyce, and 'mysterious muske'. It also has after-sun moisturisers and an Aloe Vera gel to help maintain a healthy tan. Take the factory tour and mix your own fragrance.

The Perfume Bar on Paradise Island has not only the classic fragrances of Chanel and Yves St-Laurent, but is also the exclusive retailer of Boucheron and Clarins skin care products and makeup for the Bahamas.

Alcohol

Wholesale Wines and Spirits is on Nassau's Robinson Road, next to the Marathon Mall. Names such as Bailey's Irish Cream, Hennessy Cognac as well as the domestic brands are available at prices substantially lower than in the US and Canada.

Sweaters and Special Souvenirs

The Nassau Shop has a wall-to-wall selection of fine Irish and British woollen sweaters and scarves. Look for Pringle sweaters and other ready-to-wear fashions. Paperweights made locally from authentic Bahamian stamps depict some of the flora and fauna and historical scenes native to the islands. These reasonably-priced souvenirs can be found in Nassau at Coin of the Realm, Bernard's, and Marlborough Antiques.

Mounted coin

The Pipe of Peace, on Nassau's Bay Street, has a fine selection of imported tobaccos, cigars, film, and Polaroid cameras.

Coin of the Realm on Charlotte Street has an extensive collection of gold coins from the Bahamas and all over the world. The company can mount almost any coin and it can be put on a 14K or 18K gold or sterling silver chain.

Eating Out

The variety of Bahamian restaurants is very much geared to the tourist economy. You can get anything from sushi to schnitzel here, not forgetting the staple McDonald's and Wendy's, but don't pass up the Bahamian home cooking which is to be found in even the most touristy local restaurants.

Prices here are about the same as in any American city – local Bahamian restaurants tend to be cheaper and can range from gourmet to genuine native speciality. A 15 percent tip is considered standard for good service. Most restaurants and bars automatically add it to the bill. Ask if you're not sure.

Stuffed grouper

A traditional Bahamian breakfast is boiled fish and johnny cake. The fish is usually fresh-caught grouper – a firm, white fish that tastes somewhere between sole and crab. It is boiled, with a few pieces of potato and some onions, salt and peppercorns. The baked johnny cake is really a sweet-tasting cornbread, served hot from the oven. North America's influence has also put eggs and bacon on most menus, though grits (mashed corn) are easily substituted for the bacon.

Conch ('conk') meat, taken from the shellfish of the same name, is the national seafood. Conch salad is usually the raw conch, chopped, with onion, green pepper, and fresh tomato, and marinated in lime juice. Variations include baked, fried, or 'steamed' conch – morsels sauteed in a tomato-based sauce, loaded with onions, green peppers and subtle spices. Grouper, snapper, lobster (crayfish) are usually accompanied by brown pigeon peas and rice.

More chicken is eaten than any other meat including seafood, probably because the sea produce fetches a good price as export. Peas and rice and potato or macaroni salad make up the side dishes.

Desserts may be a huge slab of chocolate cake or hot apple pie. Don't pass up the homemade lemon or lime pie, though; it is made from local fruit, and has just the right sweet-tart taste. For a truly decadent experience, try the guava duff.

In the following listings, meals up to $10 per person are considered to be inexpensive, $10–20 moderate, $20–30 above average, over $30 expensive.

New Providence and Paradise Island

BUENA VISTA
Delancey Street
Tel: 322-2811
Built in the 1800s, this renovated mansion in Nassau's downtown area has Continental and Bahamian selections on its menu, as well as the Vintage Club, with an excellent in-house jazz combo. Open at 6pm, it serves dinner from 7pm. Closed Sunday. Reservations advised. *Above average.*

Bahamian buffet

CAFE JOHNNY CANOE
Nassau Country Club
West Bay Street
Tel: 327-3373
A unique ambiance is created by the native wood, photos of old Nassau, and original Bahamian art, at this, one of Nassau's newest restaurants. Located on the Cable Beach strip, it has an excellent breakfast, lunch, and dinner menu. Service is exceptional, and there's live music and a junkanoo 'rush' every evening. *Moderate.*

CLUB LAND'OR BLUE LAGOON RESTAURANT AND LOUNGE
Paradise Island
Tel: 363-2400/2
See the stars through the stained-glass ceiling. Complimentary hors-d'oeuvres. Romantic candlelight, native seafood and international cuisine. Dance to a live band after dinner, served from 5–10pm. *Above average.*

Graycliffe: a 250-year-old estate

COCONUTS–HOME OF LE SHACK
East Bay Street
Tel: 325-2148
This is really two restaurants with the same management. The indoor Coconuts serves beef and seafood, with crystal water glasses and linen tablecloths. Step outside to the deck of Le Shack, which overlooks Nassau Harbour, and munch on hearty hamburgers and fries under your own thatched gazebo. Live entertainment on weekends. Open from 11am, with Happy Hour Monday through Friday from 5–7pm. *Moderate.*

GRAYCLIFFE
West Hill Street
Tel: 322-2796
The Bahamas' only 5-star restaurant. From the tuxedoed livery man who opens your car door, to the Baccarat crystal and world-famous wine cellar of the 250-year old estate, it's easy to see why it was rated one of the world's top 10 restaurants by *Lifestyles of the Rich and Famous*. Though pricey – about $100 per person, the food, the service, and the ambiance are unforgettable. Dinner served from 6pm. *Expensive.*

An ocean view at Traveller's Rest

MAIN STREET CAFETERIA
Shirley Street Plaza
Tel: 393-4473
This establishment offers an all-Bahamian menu of meats, fish, and local vegetables, served cafeteria-style. You can eat in or takeout. It is conveniently located by the Paradise Island Bridge, near the corner of Shirley and Mackey streets. *Inexpensive.*

SEASIDE BUFFET
Carnival's Crystal Palace and Casino
Cable Beach
Tel: 327-6200
In an advantageous location just opposite the casino. There are international and Bahamian selections at the gigantic breakfast, lunch, and dinner buffet – complete with a three-tiered dessert section – which make it easily the best bargain on the island for the truly hungry tourist. Open from 7am–4am. Dress is casual. *Moderate to above average.*

STEFANIA'S CAPRICCIO
Cable Beach
Tel: 327-8547
Authentic Italian specialities, ranging from their homemade ice-cream to pasta and desserts. The tiny cafe has checkered tablecloths, flowers at the table, and cheery service at modest rates. *Moderate.*

Fatman's Nephew

TRAVELLER'S REST
West Bay Street
Gambier Village
Tel: 327-7633
I give this place top marks for informal island atmosphere. With the best banana Daiquiri on the island, it has an excellent Bahamian menu to match the ocean view from the patio. Open 11am to 11pm. *Moderate.*

Grand Bahama

BUCCANEER CLUB
Deadman's Reef
Tel: 352-5748
With its own beach, it offers complimentary fritters, reasonable prices, and excellent Swiss-Bahamian cuisine. Food is either buffet or à la carte. *Above average.*

MR BAKER
East Mall Drive (opposite Freeport Inn) downtown
Tel: 352-8666
Their coffee shop serves Bahamian breakfasts from 7am onwards. Also serves lunch, but the real draw is fresh breads and pastries. *Inexpensive.*

FATMAN'S NEPHEW
Port Lucaya Marketplace
Tel: 373-8520
Prepares grilled fish to order and a selection of American and Bahamian cuisine. *Moderate.*

Try for a ringside seat at Pier One Restaurant

PIER ONE
Freeport Harbour
Tel: 352-6674
Sharks provide the floor show here. Excellent seafood. *Expensive.*

PUB ON THE MALL
Opposite International Bazaar
Tel: 352-5110
Home of Freeport's oldest and most authentic English-style pub. Also has a superb Italian restaurant as well as a funkily-designed grill room and rotisserie. *Moderate.*

Eleuthera

BUCCANEER CLUB
Governor's Harbour, central
Tel: 332-2500
Try their Conch Creole special. They also serve sandwiches and light lunches. (Note: Credit cards not accepted here.) *Moderate.*

CAMBRIDGE VILLAS
Gregory Town
Tel: 332-0080
Best meal deal on the island, with extraordinary conch chowder served with hot homemade bread. Open for breakfast, lunch and dinner. *Moderate.*

HARBOUR LOUNGE
Harbour Island
Tel: 333-2031
Located under the fig tree by the waterfront and within walking distance of the straw market. Try the 'five-in-one' soup, or grilled chicken. *Inexpensive.*

MATE AND JENNY'S
Palmetto Point
Tel: 332-2504
Serves lunch and dinner, but make the trip just for the homemade pizza. *Inexpensive.*

SEA GRAPE RESTAURANT AND BAR
Spanish Wells
Tel: 333-4371
Either dine indoors or on the patio bar. Emphasis tends to be on the day's fresh catch of fish, but Bahamian beef and chicken dishes are also available. *Moderate.*

Pineapple pastries

Nightlife

The most readily available entertainment on New Providence and Grand Bahama are the casinos, of course. Even if you don't think of yourself as the gambling type, you really shouldn't pass up experiencing the electricity in the air as the dice roll and the bets are being made – from the 5-cent one-armed bandit, to the minimum $400-bet baccarat table. Besides, where there's a casino, you can be sure there's a disco, casino show, and live band close by.

Bahamians take their culture seriously, and are prolific and professional when it comes to live performances. Check the theatre listings, or with the Ministry of Tourism, to find out where and what is happening. This will include not only original plays and musicals, but also amateur and professional dance ensembles. If you can get a ticket, you'll be in for a world-class performance at ridiculously inexpensive ticket prices.

The range of evening activities is decidedly smaller in the Family Islands, where a night on the town will only be on weekends, and most likely at a hotel bar. Fortunately, that's the charm of true island living, and a game of dominoes or billiards at a tiny bar can become a wonderful memory. The few discotheques and nightclubs are those who get locals as their repeat customers, rather than catering to a fast tourist turnover. What they don't have in glitz and high-tech, they more than make up for in island hospitality.

Each of the daily newspapers on New Providence and Grand Bahama has an entertainment section which is regularly updated. The *What to Do* book (Dupuch Publications), overflows with nightclubs, evening sports competitions, and concert and cabaret venues.

It includes most Family Island nightspots, too. A Ministry of Tourism Office is on every island; representatives are knowledgeable and friendly, and will go the extra mile to ensure your needs are met.

Carnival's Crystal Palace

Nassau as night falls

Cruises

EVENING DINNER CRUISE
Calypso I and Calypso II, Paradise Island Terminal, Paradise Island
Tel: 363-3577
Hop on board and cruise to secluded Blue Lagoon Island for a romantic, 3-hour dinner cruise. Calypso entertainment is performed by a live band. Cruise is 7–10pm. Reservations advised.

Bars

ATLANTIK BEACH RESORT
Lucaya, Grand Bahama
Tel: 373-1444
Enjoy delicious cocktails as you listen to soft piano music.

ED AND MARIO'S RESTAURANT AND BAR
West Bay Street, Nassau
Tel: 322-4792
Enjoy some homemade pizza or pasta while playing the island's only interactive trivia video game. There are prizes and cash giveaways every night, as guests compete against other players in the lounge and abroad.

TAMARIND HILL RESTAURANT AND MUSIC BAR
Village Road, Nassau
Tel: 393-1306
An acoustic duet sings old-time calypso melodies and more recent soft-rock of James Taylor, Simon and Garfunkel and other favourites.

Jazz

THE VINTAGE CLUB
Buena Vista Restaurant
Nassau
Tel: 322-2811
A contemporary jazz combo performs in a bistro atmosphere. Bar opens at 6pm.

CAFE DE PARIS
Le Meridien Royal Bahamian
West Bay Street
Nassau
Tel: 327-6400
Features the island's only Sunday 'Jazz Brunch'. Enjoy music by Nassau's best live soft-jazz musicians while partaking of a delectable selection of dishes from a 40-ft (12-m) long buffet table loaded with everything from smoked salmon to fresh island fruits.

Cocktail
Cabaret / Revues

THE PALACE THEATRE
*Carnival's Crystal Palace Resort
and Casino
Nassau
Tel: 327-6200*
Experience *Jubilation* in the 800-seat Palace Theatre. The show has high-kicking, fast-paced dance numbers, glitzy costumes and even live Bengal tigers that will disappear before your very eyes. Choose either the cocktail or full dinner show. Reservations are strongly advised.

LE CABARET THEATRE
*Paradise Island Casino
Paradise Island
Tel: 363-2222*
Glittering sets, shining costumes, beautiful showgirls. Nightly cocktail and dinner shows.

Live Calypso

COCONUTS/HOME OF LE SHACK
*East Bay Street
Nassau
Tel: 325-2148*
There is a live calypso band every Friday and Saturday evening.

PICK-A-DILLY
*The Parliament Hotel
18 Parliament Street
Nassau
Tel: 322-2836/7*
The in-house band called Night Watch performs nightly.

PORT LUCAYA MARKETPLACE
*Lucaya
Grand Bahama*
There's free live entertainment at the Centre Bandstand on the waterfront from 8pm to midnight. During the week there is calypso and *soca*, and on Sunday during the late afternoon there are gospel performances by local and international groups.

CASINO ROYALE ROOM
*Princess Casino
Freeport
Tel: 352-7811*
This is a 2-hour cabaret show, featuring French cancan dancing.

FLAMINGO SHOWCASE THEATRE
*Lucayan Beach Resort and Casino
Grand Bahama
Tel: 373-7777*
The 'Little Darlin' rock and roll revue features music from the 1950s and 1960s, in a Vegas-style revue.

Sing-alongs

PLUMES
*The Sheraton Grand Hotel lobby bar
Paradise Island
Tel: 363-2011*
Guests are invited to sing along with the pianist while enjoying their favourite drinks at Happy Hour prices. From 5–7pm nightly.

THE SPORTS BAR
beside Paradise Island Casino
Paradise Island
Yes, we have karaoke ! Complete with fully orchestrated background music, voice enhancement, easy-to-read lyrics. Every Monday and Thursday 7-10pm.

Native Shows

PEANUT TAYLOR'S DRUMBEAT CLUB
West Bay Street
Nassau
Tel: 322-4233
The original all-Bahamian supper club revue, with junkanoo drumming, fire and limbo dancing, ,and a female impersonator. Not to be missed. Reservations advised.

TRADEWINDS LOUNGE
Paradise Island Resort and Casino
Paradise Island
Tel: 363-3000
The club has a Bahamian musical revue, limbo and fire dancers, and a Wednesday night junkanoo festival.

Discotheques

CAMBRIDGE VILLAS
Gregory Town
Eleuthera
Tel: 332-0080
Locals come from all over the island to show off the latest dance steps for the disco weekends, Thursday to Sunday evening. Dress casual and be prepared to dance till dawn.

LE PAON
Sheraton Grand Hotel
Paradise Island
Tel: 363-2011
With four different dance areas, it features sounds of the 1950s and 1960s, calypso, local and other Caribbean music. All of this comes with a breathtaking panoramic ocean view.

CLUB FANTA-Z
Crystal Palace Resort and Casino
Nassau
Tel: 327-6200
Hotel guests taking a break from the casino can 'boogie on down' under flashing neon lights and the latest tunes. Open until 4am.

Boogying Bahamian style

CLUB PASTICHE
beside Paradise Island Casino
Paradise Island
Tel: 363-3000
Very popular with the locals, this club features the latest disco hits.

Theatres

DUNDAS CENTRE FOR THE PERFORMING ARTS
Mackey Street
Nassau
Tel: 393-3728
Comparable in quality to Broadway, but in a more intimate venue. Call to find out what's in repertory.

REGENCY THEATRE
Freeport
Grand Bahama
Tel: 352-5533
'Friends of the Arts' put on original plays, and sponsor guest performers from abroad.

Calendar of Special Events

New Year's Day, a public holiday, truly begins at 4am in Nassau, Freeport and almost all the Family Islands. In the open-air Junkanoo Competition, groups dressed in colourful costumes of crepe paper vie for cash awards and instant fame as they 'rush' down the main streets dancing to the infectious rhythms of cowbells, goatskin drums, whistles, and homemade instruments. Many Bahamians belong to Junkanoo groups sponsored by local businesses.

Bahamas Princess $50,000 Crystal Pro-Am Golf Tournament is held in Freeport.

Court opening

Bahamas Windsurfing finals, at the Lucayan Beach Hotel, Freeport.

Changing of the Guards ceremony, Nassau. A tradition of pomp and pageantry marking the changing of the guard (the Royal Bahamas Police) at Government House, the residence of the Governor-General, who is the personal representative of Queen Elizabeth II. The ceremony takes place every second Saturday in the Government House grounds, at 10am.

Supreme Court Opening, Nassau. This picturesque ceremony opens the first quarterly session of the Bahamas Supreme Court. The Chief Justice, dressed in ceremonial robes, inspects a Royal Bahamas Police Force Guard of Honour in front of the Supreme Court building. The world-famous Police Force Band performs.

People-to-People Tea Party, Government House Ballroom, 4–5pm, the last Friday of each month. A full British tea is served to the first 200 guests, with the wife of the Governor-General in attendance.

The Bahamas National Trust Annual Open House, held at the principal agency of environmental preservation in the Bahamas, Nassau. Performances by an 'environmental' actor, garden tours, and a showcase of indigenous snakes and birds are some of the varied highlights.

Junkanoo drummer

The police force band in action

FEBRUARY / MARCH

Archives Annual Exhibition, focusing on the history of the Southern Bahamas in the foyer of the main Post Office Building, Nassau.

Annual Grand Bahama 5000 (5K) Road Race. Billed as the number one race of its kind in the Caribbean, it features world-class athletes, top local runners and walkers, and offshore participants. It has a grand opening, featuring bands, cheerleaders, bed races, and a pee wee fun run.

APRIL / MAY / JUNE

Annual International Dog Show and Obedience Trials, Nassau. Categories include hounds, sporting, toy terriers, working, non-sporting, and special 'pot cake' class. Entries from abroad are welcome.

Supreme Court Opening. See listing for January.

The Bahamas National Amateur Golf Championship, held in Lucaya, Grand Bahama. Amateurs from all of the Family Islands compete, with the winner gaining automatic membership of the Caribbean Amateur Championship team.

Labour Day, a public holiday.

Eleuthera Pineapple Festival, Gregory Town, Eleuthera. It celebrates the world's sweetest-tasting pineapple, grown on plantations throughout the island. There is a junkanoo parade, a pineapple recipe competition, various craft displays, the plaiting of the maypole, and a 'pineathelon' – a swimming, running, and cycling contest that draws an international field of competitors.

Tour de Freeport, a 100-mile (160-km) bicycle race, Freeport.

JULY / AUGUST

Annual Carib-Bahamafest Caribbean expo. An exposition showcasing the cultures and lifestyles of the Caribbean, featuring a culinary exhibition, Caribbean fashions, music and dance.

Supreme Court Opening.

Independence week celebrates the independence of the Commonwealth of the Bahamas, with a range of festivities, parades, and celebrations. On 10 July, the national holiday, at West End in Freeport there is a junkanoo parade at 4am.

The first Monday in August is a national holiday to celebrate the emancipation of slaves in 1834. The annual Fox Hill Festival, in Nassau, celebrates Emancipation over a 10-day period with a series of events including an early morning junkanoo rush-out by the Fox Hill Congos.

SEPTEMBER / OCTOBER

Annual Bahamas Jazz and Blues Festival, with international jazz and blues artists, at Paradise Island and Cable Beach.

Discovery Day Holiday, a public holiday, commemorating Columbus's discovery of Guanahani.

The annual conch-cracking competition in McCleans Town, on the eastern end of Grand Bahama.

Bahamas Futures Classic Golf Tournament, Paradise Island Golf Course.

NOVEMBER / DECEMBER

Shell Pro-Am Golf, at Paradise Island Golf Course.

Central Bank Art Exhibition and Competition. A national competition

of young artists (under 26 years) showcasing paintings and drawings in a variety of media.

Longbranch Artists and Artisan Association Annual Winter Exhibition and Sale. This is a magnificent showcase of creations in almost every pos-

A dab hand at work

sible medium plus a few surprises by artists and artisans from throughout the Bahamas.

Christmas Music Evening, held on Paradise Island, features choirs, chorales, and the Royal Bahamas Police Force Band.

Annual Renaissance Singers concert. An evening of classical, modern, and ethnic Christmas music at the Government House ballroom.

Junior Junkanoo Parade, a competitive display of indigenous junkanoo music, dance, and festive costumes by primary and secondary school students, as a prelude to the Boxing Day and New Year's Day junkanoo parades held in Nassau.

Christmas and Boxing Day, public holidays. Starting at 1am the national cultural extravaganza – junkanoo – begins. Rivalling Mardi Gras and Carnival in colours, sights, and sounds, it has to be experienced, rather than explained! Winners are announced at 8am. The junkanoo parades take place in Nassau, Freeport, and most of the Family Islands.

On the green

Practical Information

GETTING THERE

The air travel market is fiercely competitive in the Caribbean region. Fortunately, this pays big dividends to the tourist in the form of great package deals. Check with your travel agent for the best seasonal offers. Nassau International Airport on New Providence is the hub for the area, with Freeport on Grand Bahama a close second. You can get to almost any island from either of these two.

By Air

Eleuthera: Three airports serve this area and the surrounding cays: one at North Eleuthera, one at Governor's Harbour in the centre of the island, and one to the south at Rock Sound. Regular service is available from Miami on Airways International and American Eagle. Flights from Fort Lauderdale are provided by Airways International, Island Express, and US Air Express, while Bahamasair serves Eleuthera from Nassau.

Grand Bahama: Freeport International Airport is the world's largest privately-owned international airport. It has US pre-clearance facilities, and customs and immigration services 24 hours, 7 days a week. There are flights from Freeport to Fort Lauderdale, Miami, Nassau, Montreal and Toronto.

Paradise Island: Paradise Island Airways has 50-passenger, 4-engine, modern Dash 7 aircraft. It has frequent daily nonstops between Miami International, West Palm Beach, Fort Lauderdale International, and Orlando International. It is minutes to downtown Nassau and the fine resorts on Paradise Island. There are also pre-clearance facilities.

New Providence: Nassau International Airport has recently completed a $60 million airport expansion project. Its US pre-clearance and customs facility can process

Prepare for landing

Cruising into port

more than 1,200 visitors per hour, and its main terminal almost 3,000 per hour. There are flights from Nassau to Atlanta, Baltimore, Boston, Charlotte, Chicago, Cincinnati, Cleveland, Dallas, Dayton, Fort Lauderdale, Los Angeles, Miami, Nashville, Newark, New York, New Orleans, Orlando, Raleigh/Durham, West Palm Beach, Philadelphia, San Jose, San Juan, and Washington DC. Montreal and Toronto in Canada; Kingston and Montego Bay, in Jamaica; and London, England.

By Sea

Cruise travel has taken off in the Caribbean, and that includes the Bahamas. International lines dock in downtown Nassau, Freeport, and Eleuthera. If you prefer the shorter stays ashore, you might want to try some of the following companies: Royal Caribbean Cruises (*Emerald Seas*) 800-327-7373; Carnival Cruise Lines (*Carnivale, Mardi Gras, Jubilee, Fantasy*) 800-327-9501; Chandris Cruise Lines (*Galileo, Crown Del Mar*) 800-223-0848; Crown Cruise Lines (*Viking Princess*) 800-841-7447; Premier Cruises (*Dolphin*) 800-222-1003; Norwegian Caribbean Lines (*Sunward, Seaward, Norway*) 800-327-7030; Premier Cruise Lines (*Oceanic, Royale, Atlantik, Majestic*) 800-327-7113; Princess Cruises (*Star Princess*) 800-421-0522; and Royal Caribbean Cruise Lines (*Nordic Prince*) 800-327-6700.

Setting foot on shore can also be by a number of mail boats, which use Potter's Cay in Nassau as the port of entry. These include the *M/V Current Pride*, the *M/V Bahamas Daybreak II*, and the *M/V Harley* and *Charley*.

Water taxis to Spanish Wells from the Eleuthera mainland cost approximately $5 per person. From the mainland to Harbour Island is about $4 per person.

TRAVEL ESSENTIALS

When to Visit

Temperatures are moderate, at usually a low of 60°F and a high of 75°F, almost year-round. The exception are the hot summer months of July and August, when the temperature can range from 80°F to the high 90s. In general, the season is year-round, although the slowest time is September/October each year, when many of the attractions and hotels etc take the opportunity to refurbish.

Visas and Passports

Visas are not required from US citizens or citizens of British Commonwealth countries. A US birth certificate or driver's photo ID can be sufficient to get you through the customs checkpoint, but the easily recognisable passport is a sure thing, and always speedier.

Citizens of Cuba and all former Communist countries must have both passports and visas, even if visiting for only brief periods of time. This is also true for citizens of South Africa, Spain, the Dominican Republic and Haiti.

When you travel to the Bahamas from a foreign country you are given an immigration card to fill in. The immigration officer at the point of entry detaches the main part of the card and leaves you with a stub. Be sure to return the stub upon departure.

Vaccinations

Vaccination certificates are not usually required, unless you have arrived within seven days from one of the following countries: Burkina Faso, Gambia, Ghana, Nigeria, Sudan, Zaire, Bolivia, Brazil, Colombia, Peru.

Pets

Must be over 6 months of age and must have a valid import permit. Contact the Director of Agriculture, Department of Agriculture, at PO Box N-3028, Nassau, the Bahamas.

Customs

Residents from the US are allowed duty-free items valued up to $600 retail, provided they are properly declared to the

customs inspector. The duty-free exemption can be claimed once every 30 days, provided the resident has been outside the US for at least 48 hours. A family of four may take home $2,400 of duty-free goods. US residents can even take up to $1,000 above the $600 allowance by paying a flat 10 percent duty on the additional purchases. Each resident aged 21 or older can include 2 litres (67.6 oz) of alcoholic beverages if one litre is manufactured in the Bahamas or another Caribbean country. 100 cigars (not Cuban) and 200 cigarettes can be imported duty-free. There is no age limit on those purchasing cigars and cigarettes.

There is also a flat rate of $1,000 duty for a family of four, which can be grouped for a total $4,000 value for entry at the flat rate of duty; this can be applied no more than once every 30 days.

No tortoiseshell goods, plants, or fruits are allowed.

For Canadian residents, duty-free allowances depend on the time you spend outside Canada, and on previous claims for exemptions. After 48 hours' absence, any number of times a year, you may import up to CAN $100 worth of duty-free merchandise, which must be carried by hand or in your luggage. This may include 50 cigars, 200 cigarettes, 2lbs (1kg) of tobacco and 60oz (2 litres) liquor. Once every calendar year, after 7 days' absence or more, you may take home merchandise worth up to CAN $300 duty-free.

Residents of the United Kingdom may take back home with them, duty-free, up to 200 cigarettes or 100 cigarillos or 50 cigars or 250 grams of tobacco; 1 litre of alcohol over 33 percent or 2 litres not over 22 percent; 50g of perfume or 11 oz of toilet water.

Take cover at midday

Weather

The Bahamas has its own weather, unlike the rest of the Caribbean. The Gulf Stream bathes the western coast with clear, warm water, and steady tradewinds approach the shores from the southwest. The occasional shower is brief and clears quickly. As a result, temperatures seldom drop below 60°F or rise above 90°.

Clothing

A casual spring-summer wardrobe is appropriate for day or evening. You'll probably spend most days in swimwear, shorts, slacks, or jeans. Bathing suits are permitted only on beaches or around pool areas. In the evening, depending on your choice of dinner and activities, semi-formal dresses and suits will suit the mood of the casinos, elegant restaurants, and night spots. Men are expected to wear a coat and tie after 7pm at most clubs. You may want to bring a sweater for the cooler evenings of the winter.

Electricity

120-volt, 60-cycle AC Standard North American shavers, hair dryers, and other appliances can be used. British three-pin plugs will need adaptors, and appliances will need transformers.

Time Differences

The Bahamas operates on Eastern Standard Time (which is 5 hours behind Greenwich Mean Time) from October to April, then switches back to Daylight Saving Time for the remainder of the year – the same as cities such as New York and Montreal.

GETTING ACQUAINTED
Geography

The Bahamas is an archipelago encompassing 100,000sq miles (260, 000sq km), with a land area of 5,382sq miles (14,000sq km). It comprise some 700 coral-base islands plus more than 2,000 cays and rock formations. Thirty of the islands are inhabited. Technically, the Bahamas is not part of the Caribbean (as is frequently thought), but is in the Atlantic Ocean, and is bordered on the west by the Gulf Stream.

Government and Economy

The Commonwealth of the Bahamas achieved independence on 10 July, 1973. Alog the lines of the British system of government, the Bahamas has a Prime Minister, a 49-member House of Assembly (Lower House), and a 16-member Senate (Upper House). Elections must be called every 5 years. There is also a Governor-General, who is appointed as the official representative of the Queen.

Tourism is the Bahamas' leading industry, employing almost three-quarters of the population and providing close to two-thirds of the government revenue. International banking is the second biggest industry. There is no income tax; local revenue comes chiefly from import duties and annual business licence fees. Thanks to these tax breaks foreign investment on the islands is extensive.

Religion

Though the Anglican Church (Church of England) is the official church of the Bahamas, religion has a strong ecumenical history, which means faiths from Ba'hai to Catholicism, Greek Orthodox to Muslim, are well-represented. Most churches are within easy access of hotels.

Whom Do You Trust

As with all densely populated urban centres, it is wise for travellers to be cautious with personal belongings. If you are staying at a hotel, keep your passport and excess cash in a secure area, such as your hotel safe. In Nassau and Freeport especially you will notice a marked decrease in pedestrians after sunset, particularly in the downtown areas where there are few places to visit after stores close, other than restaurants. You should keep to the malls and nightclubs after dark — unless, of course, there is one of the Bahamas' many street festivals happening; these events are well-lit and well-policed and it would be a great shame to miss them.

'Down-home' and sincere neighbourliness are still the trademarks of Eleuthera and other Family Islands' hospitality. Day or night, you can feel secure walking about. Some hotels and guest houses do not even have keys for their rooms!

Population

New Providence, though one of the smaller islands of the Bahamas, is the home of the nation's capital of Nassau and holds 65 percent of the total population, with Grand Bahama and its 'second city' of Freeport claiming 15 percent. The remaining Bahamians are spread throughout the Family Islands, with the largest concentrations in Eleuthera, Long Island, and the Abacos.

'Black' in the Bahamas can mean anything from very dark to fair-skinned, as some 85 percent of the population are of mixed African descent, 12 percent are white Bahamians, and roughly 3 percent are Asian or Hispanic.

MONEY MATTERS

In New Providence and Eleuthera, banks are open Monday through Thursday from 9.30am to 3.00pm and from 9.30am to 5.00pm on Friday. Freeport banking hours are 9.00am to 1.00pm, Monday through Thursday; 9.00am to 1.00pm and 3.00pm to 5.00pm on Friday.

Currency

The only legal tender is the Bahamian dollar (B$), which is easily interchanged with the US dollar, with which it is at par. Banks and hotels can exchange other currencies at prevailing rates.

Bahamian paper money runs in half-dollar, $1, $3, $5, $10, $20, $50 and $100 bills. (See if you can get a $3 bill or the scallop-edged 10-cent piece. They make great souvenirs of your stay.)

Note: More than $10,000 in US or foreign coin, currency, travellers' cheques, etc. going into the US must be reported to customs.

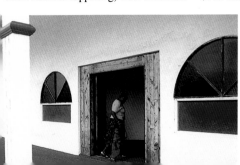

Martin church, Eight Mile Rock

GETTING AROUND

Taxis

On New Providence and Grand Bahama, the maximum taxi fares are set by government and all taxis are required to have meters in good working condition. For one or two passengers, the first quarter mile is $2. For each additional one quarter mile, add 30 cents. For each additional passenger, you pay an additional $2. There is no charge for accompanied children under three years of age. Taxis can be hired on a sightseeing basis at around $20–25 per hour, depending on the size of the cab. There is an additional charge for waiting time, at 30 cents per minute. There is no charge for up to two pieces of hand luggage, plus small bags and packages carried by the passenger. Each additional piece of luggage costs 30 cents.

On Eleuthera, as on the other Family Islands, distances between airports and accommodations vary, and most cabs no not use meters. Make sure you get a price range on transportation to and from the airport when making hotel reservations. For example, a taxi from Governor's Harbour to Cambridge Villas, in Gregory Town, is approximately $37.50 for two. It costs approximately $20 for two to get from the same airport to the Laughing Bird Apartments in Governor's Harbour, and $23.25 for two to the Rainbow Inn, in Rainbow Bay. Taxi tours are also a great way to sightsee Eleuthera, and can be arranged by your hotel or guest house.

Credit Cards and Cash Machines

Major credit cards (VISA, American Express, Mastercharge) are accepted at most stores and hotels, though you should bring your cash or traveller's cheques to the Family Islands.

There are instant teller machines on both New Providence and Grand Bahama but they will accept only Bahamian-issued bank cards.

Tipping

A 15 percent gratuity is automatic in most restaurants and bars. Waiters and waitresses, as well as taxi drivers and chambermaids, are usually given some kind of tip nonetheless.

Taxes

There is no sales tax in the Bahamas, but there is a 10 percent tax on hotel rooms in Nassau and Freeport. In the Family Islands, 10 percent is added if a hotel is a member of the Out Island Association, and 5 percent if it is not. There is a $7 ticket tax on the price of each airline or cruise ship ticket bought in the Bahamas. This is included in the price of your ticket and should not be confused with the $15 departure tax.

Money Changers

Banks are the only means by which you can change currencies. Their money-changing branches at airports and ship terminals operate during regular banking hours only. Some hotels may change limited amounts of foreign currency, but at a hefty commission. It is much easier if you come with American dollars and/or their equivalent in traveller's cheques.

Traffic cops have their work cut out

Scooters

These are available for hire at hotels and in downtown Freeport and Nassau, at about $35 for a day, or $20 for a half day. They can also be hired on Eleuthera, though they are harder to come by. A deposit is required, plus $5 for insurance. Helmets are compulsory for both driver and passenger, and swift fines are imposed for those not wearing them. Some places also hire bicycles for $10 a day, plus a $10 deposit. Whatever transport you have, don't forget to keep to the left side of the road.

Car Rental

Because of the high import taxes in the Bahamas, the rental cost may be higher than you're accustomed to – $45 a day or more. The traffic congestion in New Providence, paired with driving on the left side of the road, if you're not used to it, can make the experience pretty daunting. On such a small island there's really no need for a hired car when there are so many excellent bus and tours available.

On Grand Bahama and Eleuthera, however, having your own vehicle is the best way to capture the flavour and diversity of the islands in the time that you have. In Grand Bahama's Freeport, try Avis on 352-7666, as well as at the airport (352-7675). Grand Bahama has a well-planned highway system around Freeport and Lucaya, with never a traffic jam.

On Eleuthera the airport taxi drivers, local filling stations, and sometimes private individuals will have cars for hire, as will some local hotels. If you want to have your own transportation, ensure you have arranged a hire before you reach the island. Cars can be hired on a daily basis or by the week. Be sure to bring along a valid driver's licence.

Bus Services

The bus service in New Providence covers virtually the entire island, from dawn to dusk, and at a dollar a ride (no transfers) it is a great way to experience the local culture while seeing the sights.

In Grand Bahama, mini-buses leave from the International Bazaar for Lucaya and downtown Freeport. Even though they

Choose your transport

are public transport, the other type of buses, called jitneys, are owned by individual entrepreneurs, so you may find yourself sitting for a while waiting for the driver to get a full load. To make sure the bus is going where you want to go, ask the driver before you get on. Jitneys run from downtown Freeport to Eight Mile Rock, West End and East End. Check with the Tourist Information Centre or your hotel for more information. A complimentary bus service is provided to the beach by city hotels and by outlying hotels to Freeport.

There are no public buses on Eleuthera, though most of the hotels provide shuttle services to the local beaches and closest settlements.

HOURS AND HOLIDAYS

Business Hours

Stores are open 9.30am-5.30pm Monday through Saturday. The larger malls on New Providence and Grand Bahama are open until 8 or 9pm on weekends, and on Sunday afternoons.

Public Holidays

January, New Year's Day, Good Friday, Easter Sunday and Monday. Whit Monday, Labour Day, the first Monday in June. Independence Day is 10 July. Emancipation Day (August Monday) is the first Monday in August. 12 October is Columbus (Discovery) Day. 25 December is Christmas Day, 27 December is Boxing Day. Most stores are closed on these holidays and on Sunday, except drug stores; food stores are open from 7am to 10am.

Market Days

The straw, fruit, and fishing markets are open 7 days a week, and on most holidays as well.

ACCOMMODATION

There are 77 hotels in Nassau, 25 on Grand Bahama, and a total of 2,206 rooms 0n the Family Islands. During high season (December to April), a two-bedroom furnished suite rents from $265–550 per day on Paradise Island, and at about $295 per day in Nassau. A double room is around $90 a day in Nassau and $150 a day on Paradise Island. Package deals from Miami can slash those rates dramatically, offering 3 nights, 2 days, at as little as $200 per person.

The Modified American Plan (room, breakfast, and dinner) or European Plan (room only) is available at most hotels. On the Family Islands, double rooms are about $65 per day at the smaller hotels during high season, while the larger hotels charge about $90 per day. There is a room occupancy tax of 10 percent (4 percent levied by the government and 6 percent for hotels to fund joint promotional and advertising budgets).

In the list that follows, inexpensive rooms are those priced at less than $80 per night for a single room. Moderate prices are about $80–130 per night, Expensive $130–170; Luxury accommodations are plentiful, and range from $170 upwards.

Hotels

New Providence

MARRIOTT RESORT AND CRYSTAL PALACE CASINO
Cable Beach
Tel: 327-6200
The largest resort in the Bahamas, it has 867 guest rooms, 23 deluxe theme suites and seven suites. The casino has several restaurants, a Vegas-style dinner club, shops, and a health club. *Luxury*

CORAL WORLD HOTEL
Silver Cay
Tel: 328-1036
Located at the site of the same name, each of the 22 units here has its its own swimming pool. All suites have satellite television, VCRs and microwaves in the kitchen. *Expensive.*

LE MERIDIEN ROYAL BAHAMIAN
Cable Beach
Tel: 327-6400
The Rolls Royce of hotels, situated on Cable Beach. Secluded, sedate, old-world, tastefully-appointed, and with its own beach and gourmet chefs, it has a spa, health club, swimming pools, and lighted tennis courts for evening matches. It is a 5-minute walk away from the Crystal Palace Casino. It's worth checking with your travel agent for special deals on this place. *Expensive.*

CLUB LAND'OR
Paradise Island
On the Paradise Island Lagoon
Tel: 326-2400
With 72 rooms and apartments, it features its own disco, native show, swimming pool, bar with jazz combo. Its Blue Lagoon restaurant serves excellent seafood under attractive domed, stained-glass roof. The complex offers babysitting facilities, too. *Moderate.*

PARLIAMENT HOTEL
Parliament Street, downtown Nassau
Tel: 322-2836
In the heart of the city, its 12 rooms are above very popular Pick-A-Dilly Restaurant and Bar, just across the street from the House of Parliament. *Moderate.*

Pool at Coral World

PARADISE PARADISE
Western end of Paradise Island
Tel: 363-2541
Pristine and pink, this hotel has a laid-back atmosphere ideal for the sports enthusiast. Has private beach, free waterskiing, windsurfing, sailing, snorkelling, and bicycles. *Moderate*

TOWNE HOTEL
George Street
Tel: 322-8450
One block from Bay Street and the Straw Market, has satellite television, dining-room, bar, sun deck, swimming pool. Good rates. *Inexpensive.*

Paradise Beach

Grand Bahama

CLARION BEACH RESORT
Lucaya Beach
Tel: 362-4399
This 175-room resort offers fine dining, a variety of water resorts and tennis. Golfing is available at the Lucaya Golf and country club (officially rated PGA destination course). *Moderate.*

BELL CHANNEL CLUB
Located off Jolly Roger Drive in Lucaya
Tel: 373-2673 or 373-3801
This is an exclusive private community offering luxuriously-furnished two-bedroom townhouses and one- or three-bedroom beach villas. Special features include private patio porches, ocean and channel views, central air-conditioning, designer interiors, cable television, whirlpools, and washers and dryers. A security gate is manned 24 hours. There is a bus shuttle, a 36-slip marina, thatched beach and barbecue gazebos. *Expensive.*

CANNES VILLAGE CONDOMINIUMS
Silver Point Beach
Tel: 373-5477
or in the US (305) 931-1566
This complex has two- and three-bedroom, three-bath fully-furnished townhouses, available for rent or sale. Attractions include enclosed upper terrace, private patio and swimming pool.

LUCAYAN BEACH RESORT AND CASINO
Lucaya Beach
Tel: 373-7777
The only beachfront casino, the Lucayan Beach Resort has the Flamingo Showcase Theatre plus an international revue and live entertainment at the casino's Cabaret Bar. The complex also features a number of good quality restaurants catering to a range of moods and tastes – everything from dockside dining to fine Continental cuisine. Other special features of the resort include freshwater pools, a marina, a range of shops, and good recreational facilities. *Expensive.*

RUNNING MON MARINA AND RESORT
Located at Kell Court and Knotts Blvd
Tel: 352-6834
Fax: 352-6835
Offers 23 rooms with two double-beds, as well as eight deluxe captain's cabins which have king-sized beds. Also available is the more elaborate Admiral's Suite, which features a furnished living room, jacuzzi, kitchenette and dining area. *Moderate to expensive.*

Eleuthera

CAMBRIDGE VILLAS
Gregory Town
Tel: 335-5080
Cambridge Villas offers rooms and apartments, a popular disco and a swimming pool at very reasonable rates. Its kitchen also produces what is arguably the best conch chowder on the island. There's also a five-passenger private plane on hand which can be chartered for island-hopping excursions. Rates range from $70–100 a day. You should add around $40 per day for breakfast and dinner. *Inexpensive to moderate.*

RAINBOW INN
Hatchet Bay
Tel: 335-0294
Has 10 oceanview, circular-shaped wooden cottages, complete with kitchenettes and private sundecks. There's also a swimming pool, tennis court, and hilltop restaurant and bar. *Moderate.*

LAUGHING BIRD APARTMENTS
Governor's Harbour
Tel: 332-2012
Overlooking the Cupid's Cay section of the picture-postcard harbour, it has fully furnished efficiency apartments, and is walking distance from the harbour shops and supermarkets. Arrangements can be made for everything from shelling to golf, as well as car and scooter rentals. Rentals are from $50 (one guest) to $100 (four guests) per night with $15 for each additional guest.

VALENTINE'S YACHT CLUB AND INN
Dunmore Town
Harbour Island
Tel: 333-2638
Settled in the centre of historic and quaint Dunmore Town and surrounded by gardens, the 21-room inn has an English-style pub, water sports, boat rentals, a marina, and complete scuba-diving and snorkelling facilities. Rates from $75 to $145 a day. *Moderate to expensive.*

HEALTH & EMERGENCIES
Pharmacies
Many drugs bought over the counter are not allowed to enter the US. Check with US customs (tel: 377-8461) before purchasing any medicines.

Medical Services
First-rate medical care is available from both public and private facilities in Freeport-Lucaya, and in Nassau. Between the private Doctor's Hospital (tel: 322-8411) and the 24-hour outpatient department at the Princess Margaret Hospital (tel: 322-2861) in Nassau, most emergencies can be promptly and efficiently attended to. For a private ambulance with paramedics, call 322-2881. In Freeport,

A familiar sight

the Rand Hospital (352-6735) is fully equipped with staff and facilities. On Eleuthera, there are government clinics at each settlement, staffed with a nurse and doctor who can provide medical services at minimal fees.

In the event there is an emergency that requires particularly sophisticated technology, Air Ambulance Associates (tel: 305-776-6800) and National Air Ambulance (tel: 305-525-5538), based in Fort Lauderdale, Florida, offer emergency transportation in medically-equipped aircraft to hospitals in the United States.

COMMUNICATION AND NEWS
Post
Use only Bahamian postage stamps on your postcards (40 cents) or letters (55 cents). Stamps are available at the Main Post Office, at the top of Parliament Street, the Shirley Street Post Office, and at most Bay Street pharmacies in Nassau. There are also post offices at the International Bazaar in Freeport, and in every major settlement of the Family Islands, open from 8.30am-5.30pm, from Monday to Friday, and until 12.30pm on Saturday.

Telephone
There is a 25-cent charge for local calls. The machine will accept only Bahamian or

American 25 cent pieces. Public phones are sparse; use your hotel or ask for the closest BATELCO (Bahamas Telecommunications) station. The area code for the Bahamas is 242. A 24-hour downtown Bahamas Telecommunications office is located on East Street, in Nassau, and has fax, telephone, and telex facilities.

Media

There are morning (*The Nassau Guardian* costs 35 cents) and evening (*The Tribune* costs 50 cents) dailies on New Providence, published Monday through Saturday. Though you can try to get some from the newsstand at your hotel, or from a bookstore, they are in fairly limited supply; it's best to purchase them from the street sellers early in the morning and at around 5pm. In Freeport, the *Freeport News* is published Monday through Friday, and costs 25 cents. Each paper has comprehensive listings of entertainments, and they make great souvenirs. *What's On in Nassau* is also a very useful tourist guide.

USEFUL INFORMATION

Disabled

There is a Desk of the Disabled at the Ministry of Social Services (tel: 323-3333). Staff will be most helpful in providing information regarding specialised transport, access ramps, and special events.

Maps and Bookshops

Almost all stores in the downtown areas of Freeport and Nassau will have city maps available at the cashier's station, as will the hotels. Also available are *What To Do* and *Best Buys* – free pocket shopping guides with maps of the local shops, as well as discount savings coupons for most of the stores advertised. They are updated regularly, and are a comprehensive and colourful tourist's friend.

The Island Shop, located in the heart of downtown Nassau, opposite the Straw Market, has the most comprehensive selection of magazines, newspapers, novels, and other reading material, including a wide selection of Bahamian works.

The BAA (Bahamas Anglo-American) Shop, farther down on Bay Street, and

Lee's Book Centre, on Parliament Street, are a few of the easy-access, smaller bookstores that offer a diverse selection of local and foreign publications.

Diving

If you are a scuba-diver be sure to bring your certification card with you, as dive operators will not allow you to dive or purchase air fills without it. It's also a good idea to bring along your log book, to document how extensive your diving experience is.

Enter another world

Language

English is spoken, with a touch of British influence in inflection and spelling. You will also notice a lilt of Bahamian dialect, influenced from African, Spanish and Indian ancestry.

Sport

In the land of endless summer you can be sure that wherever there are a few patches of open ground, there'll be a sports event in progress. Day and evening events are a daily source of entertainment, and are a great way to experience local culture. Although tradition names cricket as the of-

Beware: golf carts

ficial sport of the Bahamas, the sea remains king, as the numerous yacht and sailing regattas attest.

On land, basketball is king, though softball and soccer have recently experienced a rebirth. Outside the Bahamas, the toll free Bahamas Sports Information Centre, at (800) 32-SPORT can give up-to-date listings of events. Information can also be had from the Ministry of Youth and Personal Development, at (242) 394-0445, or the major sports complex, the Queen Elizabeth Sports Centre (tel: 323-5163).

Useful Telephone Numbers

Bahamas Tourist Offices
Duty-free information, tel: 394-3575
Ministry of Tourism General Information, tel: 322-7500/4 or Hot Line 325-4161
Long-distance operator: 0
People-to-People, tel: 326-5371
Post Office, tel: 322-3025

Time: 917
Weather: 915
Police and/or Fire Emergency: 919

Eleuthera

Governor's Harbour Police, tel: 332-2111
Medical Clinic, tel: 332-201/2774
Harbour Island Police, tel: 333-2111
Medical Clinic, tel: 333-2227
Spanish Wells Police, tel: 333-4030

FURTHER READING

Bahamas Handbook and Businessman's Annual Nassau (Etienne Supuch, Jr Publications, updated annually)

Modern Bahamian Society by Collinwood and Dodge (Ed) (Caribbean books, PO Box H, Parkersberg, IA 50665, USA)

The Bahamas: A Family of Islands by Gail Saunders (Macmillan Caribbean)

Inside Grand Bahama by Dan Buettner (Fair Prospect Press, PO Box 77033, Atlanta, Georgia 3035, USA)

The Ephemeral Islands: A Natural History of the Bahamas by David G Campbell (Macmillan Education, London, 1978)

Insight Guide: Bahamas (Apa Publications,1993)

Paradise Island Story by Paul Albury (Macmillan Caribbean)

An Economic History of the Bahamas by Anthony Thompson (Nassau: Commonwealth Publishers)

Nassau Harbour at Sunset

Index

ACKNOWLEDGMENTS

Photography Bob Friel *and*
12T, 13 Bahamas Historical Society
11, 12B & 16T Bahamas News Bureau
10, 14 Balmain Antiques
15 Stanley Toogood

Handwriting V Barl
Cover Design Klaus Geisler
Cartography Berndtson & Berndtson
Production Editor Mohammed Dar

nsight Guides

over every major destination in every continent.

Bhutan★
Boston★
British Columbia★
Brittany★
Brussels★
Budapest & Surroundings★
Canton★
Chiang Mai★
Chicago★
Corsica★
Costa Blanca★
Costa Brava★
Costa del Sol/Marbella★
Costa Rica★
Crete★
Denmark★
Fiji★
Florence★
Florida★
Florida Keys★
French Riviera★
Gran Canaria★
Hawaii★
Hong Kong★
Hungary
Ibiza★
Ireland★
Ireland's Southwest★
Israel★
Istanbul★
Jakarta★
Jamaica★
Kathmandu Bikes & Hikes★
Kenya★
Kuala Lumpur★
Lisbon★
Loire Valley★
London★
Macau
Madrid★
Malacca
Maldives
Mallorca★
Malta★
Mexico City★
Miami★
Milan★
Montreal★
Morocco★
Moscow
Munich★

Nepal★
New Delhi
New Orleans★
New York City★
New Zealand★
Northern California★
Oslo/Bergen★
Paris★
Penang★
Phuket★
Prague★
Provence★
Puerto Rico★
Quebec★
Rhodes★
Rome★
Sabah★
St Petersburg★
San Francisco★
Sardinia
Scotland★
Seville★
Seychelles★
Sicily★
Sikkim
Singapore★
Southeast England
Southern California★
Southern Spain★
Sri Lanka★
Sydney★
Tenerife★
Thailand★
Tibet★
Toronto★
Tunisia★
Turkish Coast★
Tuscany★
Venice★
Vienna★
Vietnam★
Yogyakarta
Yucatan Peninsula★

★ = Insight Pocket Guides with Pull out Maps

Insight Compact Guides

Algarve
Amsterdam
Bahamas
Bali
Bangkok

Barbados
Barcelona
Beijing
Belgium
Berlin
Brittany
Brussels
Budapest
Burgundy
Copenhagen
Costa Brava
Costa Rica
Crete
Cyprus
Czech Republic
Denmark
Dominican Republic
Dublin
Egypt
Finland
Florence
Gran Canaria
Greece
Holland
Hong Kong
Ireland
Israel
Italian Lakes
Italian Riviera
Jamaica
Jerusalem
Lisbon
Madeira
Mallorca
Malta
Milan
Moscow
Munich
Normandy
Norway
Paris
Poland
Portugal
Prague
Provence
Rhodes
Rome
St Petersburg
Salzburg
Singapore
Switzerland
Sydney
Tenerife
Thailand

Turkey
Turkish Coast
Tuscany
UK regional titles:
Bath & Surroundings
Cambridge & East Anglia
Cornwall
Cotswolds
Devon & Exmoor
Edinburgh
Lake District
London
New Forest
North York Moors
Northumbria
Oxford
Peak District
Scotland
Scottish Highlands
Shakespeare Country
Snowdonia
South Downs
York
Yorkshire Dales
USA regional titles:
Boston
Cape Cod
Chicago
Florida
Florida Keys
Hawaii: Maui
Hawaii: Oahu
Las Vegas
Los Angeles
Martha's Vineyard & Nantucket
New York
San Francisco
Washington D.C.
Venice
Vienna
West of Ireland

NOTES

NOTES

NOTES